COMMEN

MW01166077

SEVEN PENITENTIAL PSALMS

BY

JOHN FISHER, BISHOP OF ROCHESTER

(*First published in A.D. 1509*)

EDITED

WITH PREFACE AND GLOSSARY

BY

J. S. PHILLIMORE, M.A.

VOL. I.

Nibil Obstat:

S. GEORGIUS KIERAN HYLAND, S.T.D.,

CENSOR DEPUTATUS

Imprimatur:

GULIELMUS F. BROWN,

VICARIUS GENERALIS,

SOUTHWARCENSI.

15 Maii, 1914.

PREFACE.

In Maarten Maarten's novel, *The Healers,* a Dutch lady, who is just about to become a Catholic, is assailed, as with a final broadside, with the objection that she will be turning round and giving the lie to the whole history of her country. An enormous, oppressive consideration which perhaps reduces to terms some part at least of the vague bewilderment, the shivering diver's *malaise* who funks the plunge, which is the common and the inevitable experience of converts : inevitable, because, let reasoning lead never so straight and personal comforters be never so reassuring, that particular act of faith can never not be an act. The shock of this alteration of spiritual and intellectual climate is greater, perhaps, for a Briton or a Dutchman than for any others, just because that Revolution in the sixteenth century did so far succeed in making, for a time, the new religion overlay the whole length and breadth of public life in the nation.

A Nonconformist, it has been said (perhaps unjustly), could not write the history of England from his Nonconformist point of view, because he is foreign to it, all but a phase which came late and obtained only partially. From his point of view he cannot command the subject. The Alteration of Religion (as Cecil called it, surely knowing what he meant) in England organized a state of things by which Anglican and English should tend to become synonyms, the Establishment and the nation co-extensive, and all such persons as might refuse to accept the sovereign for their " Only Supreme Governor " in matters of religion be guilty not only of national disloyalty but of self-ostracism. "Bluff King Hal" and "Good Queen Bess" became Shibboleths. And not content with that, the omnipotent exploiters of the new system brought in the subtle forces of convention and etiquette, and "scandal about Queen Elizabeth" was not merely a phrase to discredit, unheard, any dangerous historical revisions, but a social verdict of Bad Form. The great general legend, composed gradually and in the main unconsciously, more by instinct than policy, was composed of many falsifications of detail, all directed to subserve a common bias: namely to give the "colour" (as the old rhetoricians called it) that England's greatness only began with England's Protestantism. The Renaissance, which in fact was arrested and delayed for a century by the Tudors, must (to suit the Ascendancy) be represented as a necessary and characteristic accompaniment of the new religion. English literature must begin with Elizabeth: or rather, that must be its glorious sunrise, harbingered by the glimmerings of a dawn in Wiclyf, a person about whom our evangelical mythologists have been peculiarly busy and copious. (See Gasquet's *The Old English Bible and Other Essays*.) Tennyson, a credulous poet, endowed with a journalist's sensitiveness to the fashion of his time, and in whom as in an echo we may measure the clamorous resonance of Froude's fictions, by his

        spacious times of Great Elizabeth

phrased just what many people were predisposed to believe. "Spacious times." How gratifying to national self-complacency! What did it matter if in times so spacious there should be no room for a Campion or a Southwell, except a hiding-hole, or a rack or a gibbet? Better still, the great term "Elizabethan" became serviceable for a double equivoque: thus, Elizabethan ("we always thought")=Protestant; but evidently all literature produced in the reign of Elizabeth is Elizabethan : *Ergo*, the whole glory of English literature is Protestant. In some such style are the syllogisms of prejudice constructed. And then again, as a counterpart to suppressing our Allens and Campions and Parsonses and Stapletons, they will have the word " Elizabethan ", with convenient slovenliness, used to include any such Sixteenth Century work whatsoever, as it may suit their purpose to include under any special category. Thus from the first half of that century they pilfer its songs and ballads and sweep them all into the harvest of Elizabethan (*i.e.*, Protestant, *post* Reformation) lyric.

But in the particular instances of Fisher and More a graver *suppressio veri* has been perpetrated. It has been tacitly agreed, in the interests of the Ascendancy, that these two shall be left in darkness. Their martyrdoms are lightly dismissed as regrettable but inevitable un-pleasantnesses, such as will happen in the best-regulated Reformations, and which it is bad form to make much ado about. " Oh, yes, such a pity, but of course . . . " Or, when you drive an Anglican friend into a corner by arguing that if Henry's assumption of that Only Supreme Governorship in all questions Spiritual and Ecclesiastical (to which every 'Anglican prelate to this day swears allegiance) really meant so little, then More and Fisher must have been rather idiots than martyrs, in a moment you will have him guilelessly repeating from his manuals that More and Fisher were eccentrics, doctrinaire expo-ponents of a maximist Papalism. Surely the most impudent and fatuous of lies. More, who had warned Henry that in his *Assertio* he put the Pope's prerogative rather dangerously high, to be represented as an ultramontane fanatic !

Plainly the theory of a sudden outburst and spring-time of literature, arising with the beginnings of the new religion, is sorely embarrassed if any pre-Elizabethan writer be allowed to appear eminent. More must therefore be buried in silence and obscurity; his claim to rank as the Father of English History or English Prose be hushed up, and no other work of his permitted to be spoken of but *Utopia*. *Utopia* was a youthful trifle which he lived to regret and to disown, and his esteem of which is best shewn by the fact that he never put it into English. The young student who swallows what his handbooks tell him is never allowed to suspect that More's English works fill 1400 pages of folio. Or suppose him to have learned this much (for the literary histories mention it), he is little the forwarder. There is hardly a possibility of his reading them. Since 1557 there has never been a complete reprint; and only three pieces, I think, have been reprinted at all.[1]

The famous series which has done so much for the revival of forgotten worthies and re-opened so many choked sources of English, Arber's Reprints, comprised no Catholic work at all. Surely an eloquent fact, and in itself a clinching proof that the Ascendancy has pursued the policy of choking as well as of poisoning the wells of history. If Fisher had been a heretic, you may be sure Arber would have included these Sermons in the series, which contains plenty of stuff inferior to Fisher whether in point of literary merit or of historical significance in the development of style. The bibliography of

---

[1] Here is an example of the kind of thing that might make one despair. A master of English, discoursing on style and sketching an English Library, "excludes from consideration works whose sole importance is that they form a link in the chain of development. For example, nearly all the productions of authors between Chaucer and the beginning of the Elizabethan period, such as Gower, Hoccleve and Skelton, whose works, for sufficient reason, are read only by professors and students who mean to be professors."—Arnold Bennett, *Literary Taste*, p. 90: London, 1911.

wood, 1900), as ungrudgingly fair. But the extremely inconvenient form in which alone Fisher could be read must hinder even expert English scholars from savouring quite freely and simply the racy turns and living cadences which hide themselves within a strange spelling and a dead punctuation. Such a presentment is not level with our senses.

But now some Catholics may say, "Why not let it alone? Why rake up literary antiques and curios when the Second Spring has a literature of its own, and, in particular, an abundant devotional literature of its own?" Well, we build new churches of our own because our fathers were expropriated from the old; yet, thank God, the history of ecclesiastical architecture is Catholic history beyond the power of sophistry to distort. But what would not Protestantism give to be able to claim any inheritance in Catholic art? And why should we make them a present of Literature? Is it not of great importance to the reassertion of the Church in this country that we can claim a share at all points in the national heritage? From that we can refuse to be expropriated. We have names enough to keep a footing, even during the 100 years when Anglican and English looked most like becoming synonyms, before the thin overlay of the new religion had shrunk much: Crashaw, Dryden and Pope. The Church cannot afford to yield the pen any more than the sword, to be misused. How immensely less would Newman's effectiveness have been had his literary power been negligible and his appeal restricted to an audience of *cognoscenti* in controversy or in theology!

This treatise is offered to the public which reads the Catholic Library both as an excellent piece of devotional reading and as an excellent piece of literature, deeply interesting to anybody who takes any pride in his mother tongue, and feels an honest complacency in recognizing how near to the perfect adequacy and aptness of a civilized language was the speech of our ancestors 400 years ago.

As a book of devotion it certainly escapes the commonest fault in that kind, the sin of sweetishness or false unction. The reason why this so often defaces books of devotion is that they are taken from foreign originals with too little respect for idiom. Much sentiment is good and pleasant to the native palate in French or Italian, which, done into English, will estrange, offend and even scandalize an English reader. The literary charm, the raciness, the solidity and sincerity of Fisher's English give a most engaging address to these printed missionaries. Reading and rereading these proofs I find him, in my own experience, extraordinarily satisfying and uncloying. Such sweetness without sentimentality, such mastery in tempering hope and fear together, rebuke and consolation; in a word, such a man, and such a Saint.

Moreover, is it mere antiquarianism of temper if of two books of devotion, otherwise equally good, I find that the one which is 400 years old has a seniority of values and interest to which even the modern classic must defer? History is everywhere, if you are on the alert for her: and every book has, beyond its intrinsic quality, a further quality as being a piece or a document of the mind of its time. What was our countrymen's mind like in the fatal half-century before the apostasy? You may learn it from descriptions by historians, if you please to take their word for it, but unless you know what books any generation of men read and took pleasure in, the mind of that time is closed to you. In reading this Treatise, both the preacher and his hearers revive and advance towards us and draw near out of their dim distance. Also, if I mistake not, the reader of these sermons will feel not only " How Catholic this is," but " How racy, how English this is." *Quod semper, quod ab omnibus* is a great text for many applications: let us apply it to our countrymen, and rejoice in the real continuity which makes this Doctor and Martyr such near neighbours to ourselves in the idiom and the rhythm of his language.

The taunt of the " Italian Mission " is one of those foolish taunts which blacken the utterer's lips without hitting their object. But Continuitarianism is still amongst us, the sorry remnant of false reasoning, false history and sophistication with which those who made the *gran rifiuto* after the Oxford Movement corrupted such provinces of the Victorian mind as they had access to. Now every well chosen reprint of a pre-Reformation piece of English Literature is both a sound defence against the ultra-Protestant policy of expatriating the Papists from their birthright in the national tradition, and also a demonstration of the living continuity (to take our particular case) between the Church of which the Bishop of Rochester was a Cardinal and the Church which has raised Blessed John Fisher to the honours of her altars.

It has been mentioned above that these sermons have been twice reprinted; but each time it was under conditions which leave this present book virtually unforestalled.

In 1876 Professor J. E. B. Mayor, of St. John's College, Cambridge, reprinted for the Early English Text Society, vol. i. of Fisher's Works, containing, besides this treatise, several other pieces which it is hoped also to include later in the Catholic Library. He anticipated in his advertisement that he would never finish the edition; which neither he did, nor has any other come forward to do vol. ii., using the indications which Mayor left for his eventual successor. Mayor printed from the MSS., reproducing the spelling and punctuation that he found. He was a skilled palaeographer and textual scholar, and his general accuracy beyond question; but there are nevertheless a good few passages where he makes Fisher talk nonsense, for want of some slight emendation such as he would never have stuck at had he been dealing with the text of Juvenal or Cicero. I have been content to correct these places tacitly. But the reason why his edition (not a common book, either, for that matter) is useless for all but lexicographers and (to recite Arnold Bennett's cheerless classification) "professors and students who mean to be professors," is that he meticulously preserves the ancient spelling and punctuation. Possibly Mayor would not have cared to see this papistical treatise save in the hands of antiquaries or curious *savants*. While he was about it, Gothic type would have improved the uncouthness. But certainly, as it is, no further obstacles are needed to make the book unreadable, in any effective sense of the verb to read. The modern eye cannot travel freely, picking up its clues on the page, where even the commonest word is an orthographical monster, and the stops give no clue to the articulation of the sentence. In this respect Mayor's text is a monument of laborious pedantry. Consider this phrase for example:

"Every one of them wolde execute all *that* perteyneth to his office quykly without fayninge or parcyalyte."

It looks a queer enough collection of beasts to set on a modern page, and one takes some little thought to discover what "quykly" and "parcyalyte" may mean. Show this to the railway traveller at the bookstall, and his shilling will not rise to such a bait with much eagerness. Yet nothing is amiss with it but the disguise. Put it in modern form:

" Every one of them would execute all that per-
taineth to his office quickly without feigning or par-
tiality,"
and nothing is left that need disconcert an ordinarily
literate reader. All that outlandishness, all that air as
of some quaint half-real thing raised up on the farther
side of a vast chasm of time, across which we have no
equal and familiar communications, is almost wholly a
matter of dressing and presenting, or, in other words,
of spelling and pointing.

Father Kenelm Vaughan saw this. He says in the
little Introduction to his reprint (Burns and Oates,
1888):

When my intention of reprinting this book was known, a
friend in the British Museum urged me to bring out a fac-
simile of the original text, written in Old English, which might
be a grateful reminiscence of those bygone days. But my aim
in the reproduction of this book is not a literary but a devotional one. My desire is not to gratify the tastes of antiquarians,
which has already been done by the E.E.T.S., but to supply
holy reading.

But since the present editor is aiming at an object which
lies between that and Mayor's, a middle way has been
taken here with the problem, how to present the text.
Mayor's method we have seen; this is how Father
Vaughan describes his:

Upon this edition (which I have compared with the original),
published in 1714 and modernized then to suit the requirements
of those days, I have formed this new edition, modernizing it
still further, so as to bring it down to our times. In other words
I have paragraphed these sermons, which scarcely had a break
in them from beginning to end; disentangled and divided long
involved sentences; adopted throughout modern orthography
and punctuation; replaced obsolete words with words of common
usage; and modified certain rude modes of expression, which,
though suitable to a less polished age, would grate offensively
on the ears of this more refined and sensitive generation.

All this was quite legitimate for Father Vaughan's purpose, but it transmogrifies Fisher too much for mine, for, desiring to make a reprint which should come in handy to serve the literary student's turn, who might care to read a good book of 1508, although he had no liking for a book of devotions, it would be a fatal blunder to modernize beyond the minimum point of convenience, or to bowdlerize. A true student's temper must always be what Pliny expressed: *ea est stomachi mea natura ut nil nisi merum et totum velit.*

I have therefore adapted the spelling, but not the diction, preferring instead to add a running glossary of the obsolete words, which are surprisingly few. As to Father K. Vaughan's last matter I have ventured to leave to the *Beatus* this uncloaked homeliness of his plain-speaking. I feel that one must gravely falsify either More or Fisher by dissembling a certain crudeness, profoundly and instinctively healthy; which, if we find it offensive, is just the measure of our decadence. The most vicious ages and the most vicious books taboo the *gros mot;* but there are much more insidious corruptions in the refinements of euphemists than in the round terms which More and Fisher, like St. Augustine and St. Jerome, think it no shame to write. There are Saints who have almost a cynical brusqueness in this matter, just because they hold the flesh in contempt, and grudge under its wearisome exactions. Why then should they flatter it with daintinesses of language?

I have thought it needless to say anything of Blessed John Fisher's life and martyrdom, because Father Bridgett's book is so well-known and so accessible. But in conclusion I will add two quotations. The first shall be from the Proemial Annotations upon the Psalms in the Douay Bible (*ed.* 1610):

In Litanies and almost all Public Prayers, and in administra-

PREFACE

tion of other Sacraments and Sacramentals, either whole Psalms or frequent verses are inserted. Likewise the greatest part of the Offices of our B. Lady and for the Dead, are Psalms: beside the Seven Penitential and fifteen Gradual Psalms, at certain times. So that clergymen's holy office consisteth much in singing or reading Psalms. And therefore all Bishops especially are strictly bound by a particular Canon (*Dist.* 38 cap. *Omnes psallentes*) to be skilful in the Psalms of David: and to see that other Clergymen be well instructed therein.

Here is Fisher as the model Bishop, as he was in so many other respects; and now for Fisher as prophet: this second is from our text, in the comment on Psalm cii.:

So, good Lord, do now in like manner again with thy Church militant; change and make the soft and slippery earth into hard stones; set in thy Church strong and mighty pillars that may suffer and endure great labours, watching, poverty, thirst, hunger, cold and heat; which also shall not fear the threatings of princes, persecution, neither death but always persuade and think with themself to suffer with a good will, slanders, shame and all kinds of torments for the glory and laud of Thy Holy Name.

This prayer was spoken in the last year of Henry VII.; it was fulfilled in the author's person twenty-seven years later on Tower Hill.

June 15, 1914

BIBLIOGRAPHY.

IN place of a general bibliography it will be sufficient for the scope of this volume to refer to Henry Morley's *English Writers*, vol. vii., pp. 331—335 (published 1891), and to the standard *Life of the Blessed John Fisher, Bishop of Rochester, Cardinal of the Holy Roman Church, and Martyr under Henry VIII.*, by the Rev. T. E. Bridgett, of the Congregation of the Most Holy Redeemer. Second edition 1890. These will furnish the fullest materials.

CONTENTS.

———

This treatise concerning the fruitful sayings of David the King and Prophet in the seven Penitential Psalms, divided in Seven Sermons, was made and compiled by the Right Reverend Father in God, John Fisher, Doctor of Divinity, and Bishop of Rochester, at the exhortation and stirring of the most excellent Princess Margaret, Countess of Richmond and Derby, and mother to our Sovereign Lord King Henry the VII.

HERE BEGINNETH THE PROLOGUE.

When I advert in my remembrance the fruitful and noble translations compiled and translated in time past by many famous and excellent doctors, grounded on Scripture by high authority, the which singularly not only themself applied daily to pronounce the words of our Blessed Saviour Jesu and of many prophets and prudent ecclesiastical doctors whose minds with the grace of the Holy Ghost was spiritually illumined, but also the said doctors them endeavoured with diligent labour to put in memory by writing the said sermons to the great utility and health of the readers and hearers of the same: the which premises by me inwardly considered, for as much as I of late before the most excellent Princess Margaret, Countess of Richmond and Derby and mother unto our Sovereign Lord King Henry the Seventh, published the sayings of the holy king and prophet David of the Seven Penitential Psalms, in the which my said good and singular lady much delighted: at whose high commandment I have put the said sermons in writing for to be impressed, that all the persons that intentively read or hear them may be stirred the better to trace the way of eternal salvation, insatiately to behold with joy inestimable the glorious Trinity (Who preserve ghostly and bodily my foresaid lady and our redoubted Sovereign Lord her son with all his noble progeny!) and that the intelligents[1] of the said sermons may be gladder in the path of righteousness daily to persevere.

HERE ENDETH THE PROLOGUE.

[1] acquainted readers

B

THE FIRST PENITENTIAL PSALM.
DOMINE NE IN FURORE.

PSALM vi

FRIENDS, this day I shall not declare unto you any part of the epistle or gospel, which peradventure you do abide for to hear at this time. But at the desire and instance of them whom I may not contrary in any thing which is both according to my duty and also to their souls' health, I have taken upon me shortly to declare the First Penitential Psalm. Wherein I beseech Almighty God for His great mercy and pity so to help me this day by His grace that whatever I shall say may first be to His pleasure, to the profit of mine own wretched soul, and also for the wholesome comfort to all sinners which be repentant for their sins and hath turned themself with all their whole heart and mind unto God, the way of wickedness and sin utterly forsaken.

But or[1] we go to the declaration of this Psalm, it shall be profitable and convenient to shew who did write this Psalm, for what occasion he wrote it, and what fruit, profit, and help he obtained by the same. David, the son of Jesse, a man singularly chosen of Almighty God and endued with many great benefits; afterward he sinned full grievously against God and His law, and for the occasion of his great offence, he made this holy Psalm; and thereby got forgiveness of his sins. Behold, take heed who he was, of what stock he came that made this holy Psalm, for what occasion he made it, and what profit he obtained by the same. But these things shall be more openly declared, that each one of you may know how great a sinner this prophet was and also the greatness of his sin, that we by the example of him warned, instructed and monished, despair not in any condition, but with true penance let us ask of our blessed Lord God mercy and forgiveness. We shall perceive and know the greatness

[1] before.

of his sin so much the better and sooner, if his great
unkindness shewed against God Almighty that was so
beneficial unto him, be made open and known to us.

Jesse, the father of David, had seven sons; David
was the youngest of them all, least in personage, least set
by, and kept his father's sheep. Notwithstanding, the
goodness of Almighty God only did elect and choose him,
all his brethren reject[1] and set apart, and then commanded Samuel, the bishop and prophet, to anoint him
king of Israel. Was not this a great kindness of Almighty God shewed unto such a manner[2] vile person, set
to the office of keeping beasts, that He of His goodness
would call from so vile an office, set him by His commandment as king and head of all his people? But let
us see what did He more for him. King Saul, into whom
after the breaking of the commandment of Almighty God
entered a wicked spirit, the which troubled and vexed
him sore; and when that he made search all about for to
have a cunning and melodious harper, by whose sweet
sound (when that he should strike upon his harp) the
woodness[3] of the foresaid wicked spirit should be mitigate and suaged,[4] none such could be found but this
same David, which by a special gift of Almighty God
could play well and nobly upon the harp. At any time
when the wicked spirit vexed and troubled king Saul,
David should come before him. And as often as he
played upon his harp, both Saul was refreshed and comforted, and the wicked spirit departed and troubled him
no more for that time. Was not this a great benefit of
God given to David? And beside this, when Israel
should make battle against the Philistines, one of their
nation among them, a marvellous strong man as great
as a giant, strengthened and clad on every feature with
sure and strong armour, he called all Israel to fight
with him, man for man, under this condition, that if any
Israelite could vanquish him in battle, all the multitude
of the Philistines should be subject to Israel, and con-

---

[1] being rejected.   [2] so to speak.   [3] madness.
[4] assuaged.

trariwise if he got the victory, all Israel in like condition
should be subjugate and thrall unto the Philistines. No
man among all the great multitude of Israelites had
audacity or boldness with this monstrous creature, this
Philistine, to make battle, save only this little person
David; to whom Almighty God gave so great boldness
(although he was but little in personage and stature);
nevertheless he in no condition feared to fight and make
battle with this great and mighty giant. At the last,
though it were incredible to every man that David should
have the victory, he armed himself with the armour of
King Saul. But as a man not customed to wear harness,
he was then more unwieldy to do any feat of arms than
he was before, and could not use at liberty any member
of his body. Therefore soon he stripped him of that
array, and naked without any manner of weapon earthly
to defend himself, save only with his staff, sling and a
stone, went forth to fight with this great giant. And as
this Philistine came to himward with a cruel and a blas-
phemous countenance, he hit him at one cast with a stone
on the forehead and so overthrew him, and shortly drew
nigh him and with the sword of the same deformed creature he struck off his head. O marvellous God, by whose
only power this weak and little person David, unarmed,
obtained the great and marvellous victory of so proud an
enemy! But what of this? The benefits which Almighty
God did for him be innumerable and impossible for me
now to shew them all. He defended him against the
envious minds of his brethren. He defended him from
the dangers and perils of the two cruel beasts, the lion
and the bear. He saved him harmless from the envious
persecutions of King Saul, moreover against the hatred
of the Philistines. And at the last, when King Saul was
dead, He made him King of Israel. By these great and
manifold gifts we may understand how much David ought
to humble himself unto Almighty God and how much he
was bounden to Him. And how ungentle he ought to
be reputed and taken, if he should not serve his Lord
and Maker with all his whole mind and true heart. Furthermore, after he was made king he lived in peace and

ease, and had many wives, not content with them, set apart[1] the goodness and gentleness of Almighty God, he took to him another man's wife, and with her committed adultery, contrary to God's law. This woman was the wife to his true knight called Uriah, which at that time was in the king's wars as a valiant knight. David, then fearing that his grievous offence of adultery should be openly known, sent for Uriah, trusting verily at his coming that he would resort unto his wife; but firmly he denied it, and would not come at his sending for. Then David, seeing that, found the means by his letters sent unto Joab, the chief captain of his host, that the said Uriah should be set in the foremost ward of the battle, and so for to be slain: which according to his desire was done, and this good knight Uriah there suffered death. Behold the accumulation and heaping of sin upon sin! He was not satisfied with the great offence of adultery done against Almighty God, but shortly after committed manslaughter. Adultery in any person is to be abhorred; and it is more to be abhorred if manslaughter be joined to it; and namely[2] the slaying of so clean and so holy a man to whom he was so greatly beholden for his truth[3] and labours which he took in his wars and business. Now, moreover, how many great benefits had he before this of Almighty God, whereby he might not (of very right) break the least of His commandments without great unkindness! He nevertheless would not let[4] to commit these abominable sins, adultery and manslaughter; and, a long season, lay and was accustomed in them. But yet let us call unto our minds how merciful Almighty God was unto him for all this. Our Blessed Lord Almighty God of His infinite goodness and meekness sent a prophet unto him, the which warned him of his great offences. And as soon as David was in will for to acknowledge himself guilty, and said *Peccavi Domino:* " I have offended my Lord God," anon forthwith all his sins were forgiven. Is not the great mercy and meekness of Almighty God greatly to be magnified

---

[1] despite. [2] especially. [3] loyalty. [4] spare.

and spoken of, that He shewed to David, after so great
benefits given unto him, after his grievous offences and
very great unkindness, so soon for to give him mercy and
forgiveness? Yes truly. Yet notwithstanding for all
this, anon he forgot the goodness of Almighty God and
again fell to sin in the sin of pride, being proud of the
great number and multitude of his people, against the
commandment of the law of God: whereby all his great
unkindness before was renewed more and more. What
thing might he then trust to have but only the punishment
of God? Which he greatly fearing, was marvellously
penitent and acknowledged himself grievously to have
offended our Lord God, asking Him mercy; and made
this Psalm with great contrition and sorrow in his soul,
whereby again he obtained forgiveness. Now ye understand who made this Psalm, what occasion caused him to
write it, and what profit he got by the same.

Which of us now that were sick in any part of his
body, being in jeopardy of death, would not diligently
search for a medicine wherewith he might be healed, and
first make inquisition of him that had the same sickness
before? Would we not also put very trust and hope to
have remedy of our disease by that medicine whereby
like manner sickness and diseases were cured before?
Sith[1] we now therefore have heard tell for a truth how
greatly sick and diseased this prophet David was, not
with sickness of his body, but of his soul, and also with
what medicine he was cured and made whole, let us take
heed and use the same when we be sick in like manner
as he was, by our sins, shortly to be cured; for he was
a sinner as we be, but he did wholesome penance, making
this holy Psalm whereby he got forgiveness and was
restored to his soul's health. We in like wise by oft
saying and reading this Psalm, with a contrite heart (as
he did), asking mercy, shall without doubt purchase and
get of our best and merciful Lord God forgiveness for
our sins.

This Psalm is divided in three parts. In the first the

[1] Since.

mercy of God is asked. In the second reasons be made whereby the goodness of God should be moved to mercy. And in the third is great gladness shewed for the undoubtful obtaining of forgiveness. Although Almighty God in Himself and of His eternal being and nature is without mutability or change, yet divers affects[1] be given to Him in manner as be in man, as it might be thought: sometimes wroth, and sometimes merciful, in case He might be changed from wrath into meekness, but notwithstanding, as Saint James saith: *Apud Deum nulla transmutatio est neque vicissitudinis obumbratio:* "God is without mutability or change." He is always one. For as we see the beam that cometh from the sun, always one in itself, hurteth and grieveth the eye that is not clean and perfect, and comforteth the eye which is pure without any change of his[2] operation; so Almighty God is called grievous unto a sinner infected with the malice of sin, and meek and gentle unto the righteous man that is purged from sin. This is done without mutability in God. Truly as long as a creature continueth in the wretchedness of sin, so long shall he think that God is wroth with him; like as the eye while it is sore, so long shall the sunbeam be grievous and noisome to it, and never comfortable till the sickness and disease be done away. Therefore David considering in himself how grievously he had offended Almighty God, and that man may bear and suffer his punishment, maketh his prayer that He vouchsafe neither to punish him eternally by the pains of Hell, neither correct him by the pains of Purgatory, but to be meek and merciful to him. Three manner ways Almighty God dealeth with sinners after three divers kinds that be of them. Some manner of sinners there be that continue in their wretchedness till they die, and those Almighty God punisheth in the eternal pains of Hell; the ministers of those pains be the devils. Some manner of sinners there be that somewhat before their death hath begun to be penitent and amend their life, and these Almighty God punisheth in the pains of Purgatory;

---

[1] affections.   [2] its.

which have an end, and they be ministered by His angels. Thirdly, some there be which, by grace, in this life hath so punished themselves by penance for their offences, that they have made a sufficient recompense for them. And these Almighty God doth accept by His infinite mercy. Therefore this prophet saith: *Domine ne in furore tuo arguas me: neque in ira tua corripias me. Miserere mei Domine quoniam infirmus sum:* " Good Lord correct me not in the everlasting pains of Hell, neither punish me in the pains of Purgatory, have mercy on me good Lord for I am feeble and weak." Of a truth every man and woman shall stand before the throne of Almighty God at the Day of Judgment; and at that time such as never would be penitent for their offences in this life, shall be punished very sharply and with this most sharp and grievous word spoken of Almighty God. *Ite maledicti in ignem æternum:* " Go, ye cursed people, into the eternal fire." They shall go away from His face Whose beauty cannot be expressed, whereon the angels desireth to look and to behold it. And also they shall depart with His curse, not into a place of any pleasure, but of all displeasure and grievousness. Whither? Truly into the fire that never shall have end. For it shall be everlasting: *in ignem æternum.* Where also shall be no friendship that is comfortable, but on every side the horrible and fearful sight of devils. Almighty God saith: *Præparatus est diabolo et angelis ejus:* " That fire is prepared for the devil and his angels." Take heed with what painfulness and bitterness they shall be reproved, forsaken and punished which shall be tormented in that fire. Therefore our prophet David asketh of Almighty God to be delivered from that everlasting pain. *Domine ne in furore tuo arguas me.* In the everlasting punishment Almighty God shall be so grievous and untreatable that if all the angels and all the whole court of Heaven should pray for sinners, being in those pains of Hell, they should not be heard. Notwithstanding, He dealeth more meekly with the souls that be punished in the pains of Purgatory, for the which He heareth the prayers of good people. Else as it is written in Scripture: *Vanum esset et*

inutile pro defunctis exorare ut a peccatis solvantur: " It
were vain and unprofitable to pray for them that be dead,
to the intent they may be delivered from the pains deserved for sin." It is without doubt that God accepteth
the prayers, sacrifices, and other good works offered to
Him for the souls in Purgatory, whereby they may be
the sooner delivered from pain. Of a truth in that place
is so great acerbity of pains that no difference is between
the pains of Hell and them, but only eternity: the pains
of Hell be eternal, and the pains of Purgatory have an
end: therefore Almighty God doth punish sinners very
sharply in these pains although they have an end. And
because of that our prophet prayeth saying: *Neque in
ira tua corripias me:* " Correct me not good Lord in the
pains of Purgatory." The mercy of God is great upon
sinners which will turn them to Him by forsaking their
sins, that whereas they have deserved eternal pains, they
may change and mitigate them into temporal pains in
this life by penance, and after they be dead to make full
satisfaction in Purgatory. But since these pains be so
grievous as no tongue can tell, yet the mercy of God is
so great that if they will, in this life they may punish
themselves for their offence against Almighty God; and
He accepteth your own punishment done here (if it be
sufficient): so merciful that, anon when their souls be
departed from their bodies, they shall neither be cast
into Hell, neither into the pains of Purgatory, but without any let[1] to be in the glorious place of Heaven. Our
prophet therefore, fearing to offend Almighty God, since
that aforetime he was overcome by his own voluptuousness, now much more he dreadeth lest he fail and be
faint in himself for fear of the bitterness of these pains:
wherefore he saith: *Miserere mei, Domine, quoniam infirmus sum:* " Blessed Lord, have mercy on me, for of
myself I have no strength ": like as he might say " I was
feeble and faint in resisting my own pleasure, and much
more feeble I shall be to suffer those great pains. For
this cause, good Lord, neither punish me eternally in

---

[1] hindrance.

Hell, neither correct me in the pains of Purgatory, but accept my penance which my weakness may suffer now in this life." Blessed Lord, Thou art always good and mayst hurt no man without he himself be in the blame, not by Thy own fault. For whereas the sunbeam is comfortable to the eye that is clean and whole, and grievous to the eye which is sore and watery, there is no blame in the sun but only in the sickness that is in the eye. So where that[1] Almighty God rewardeth some with joy and some with pain, no blame is in God, but only in the sinner which is so sore infected with sin that Almighty God can do no less but punish him as long as he continueth in that sin, although Almighty God in Himself cannot be but all good. This holy prophet therefore prayeth that he may be made whole of his grievous sickness, which is sin, saying: *Sana me Domine:* "Good Lord make me whole." Truly that creature hath need for to be made whole which is so sore vexed with grievous sickness, that he utterly can find no rest in any part of his body; where also not only the members which be strong feel trouble and pain, but as well they that be feeble be troubled in like manner. It is the property of sin to infect any creature in that manner wise.[2] For as Isaie the prophet saith: *Cor impii quasi mare fervens quod quiescere non potest:* "The heart of a sinful person is like unto the troublous sea which never hath rest." What thing may be thought more troublous and more unquiet than is the sea when that it rageth? Even in like wise is the heart of a sinful person. Saint Ambrose asketh this question, as thus, "What pain is more grievous than is the wound of a man's conscience inwardly? It troubleth, it vexeth, it pricketh, it teareth, and also it crucifieth the mind, and it stirreth up-so-down[3] the memory, it confoundeth the reason, it crooketh the will, and unquieteth the soul." Therefore our prophet addeth in his prayer: *Quoniam conturbata sunt omnia ossa mea, et anima mea turbata est valde:* "Lord make me whole, for all the parts of my body be without rest, and my soul is sore troubled." Whereof cometh this great trouble but only of sin, which

---

[1] whereas.   [2] sort of way.   [3] upside-down.

turneth away the face of God from sinners? We read in Scripture that on a time the sea was very troublous, whilst our Saviour Jesus Christ once slept in a ship; all the sea was moved and stirred with stormy tempests, but, anon as He opened His eyes, with one word it was suaged and at rest. Which trouble and unquietness of the sea signi-fyeth the trouble of the soul when Almighty God turneth away His face from the sinner, for it is written in another place: *Avertente te faciem tuam turbabuntur:* "When thou, good Lord, turnest away Thy face all things shall be troubled." Therefore the vexation of the soul shall not be mitigate and done away until the time our merciful Lord God turn Himself unto the sinner. Our Lord shall turn Himself as soon as the sinner will be converted from his sinful life. He promised so to do by His prophet Zachary, saying: *Convertimini ad me et ego convertar ad vos:* "Be ye turned to Me, and I shall be turned unto you." O Blessed Lord, how ready is Thy mercy to sin-ners which will turn them to Thee by doing penance, that Thou would vouchsafe to promise Thyself to be turned to them as soon as they shall turn themselves unto Thee! Therefore our prophet saith to Thee: *Sed tu, Domine, usquequo?* "Good Lord why tarriest Thou so long?" As he might say: "Thou knowest my tribulation, and now I am turned to Thee; why sufferest me so long to be vexed with this trouble? Command the winds, suage the tempests, deliver my soul from these storms, for if Thy meekness be turned and look upon me, all the mem-bers of my body and also my soul shall be in rest and peace." *Convertere ergo, Domine, et eripe animam meam:* "Therefore, good Lord, be Thou turned unto me, and deliver my soul from this tribulation wherewith it is troubled by reason of my sin. Deliver my soul, make it whole from the sickness of sin by the medicine of penance, deliver it from the bitter pains of Purgatory, deliver it also from the eternal punishment which shall be exercised in Hell." This holy prophet meekly prayeth Almighty God for to be delivered from all these pains. He saith: *Salvum me fac:* "Good Lord, save me from all these outrageous pains."

All this while it hath been spoken to you of this holy prophet's petition. Now followeth the reasons which he made, whereby Almighty God must needs be moved to grant his petition. The first reason is taken of the mercy of God. But what shall we say of this? Is Almighty God unmeek and unmerciful? Nay verily. It is written by the prophet: *Misericors et miserator Dominus, patiens et multum misericors:* "Our Lord is both merciful inward and also the doer of mercy outward, patient and always merciful." He therefore hath mercy and pity upon wretched sinners, and is also much merciful; and He that is much merciful must needs exercise His mercy in deed. But upon whom? Upon righteous people? What needeth that, since in them is no wretchedness? For why? They be without sin, which only is wretchedness. Therefore to be merciful and exercise mercy in deed is necessary to sinners. The rich man oweth of duty to do his mercy upon the poor creature, and the physician upon the sick. So Almighty God must do His deed of mercy unto sinners. It is written in the Gospel: *Non iis qui sani sunt opus est medico, sed qui male se habent:* "He that be whole needeth no physician, but a physician is needful unto them that be sick." The miserable sinners which be thrust down by the most miserable sickness of sin have great need of a medicine to make them whole. What is that? Truly the mercy of Almighty God for the poorer that a man be, the more need he hath to the rich man; and the more sick that a man is, the better medicine he hath need of. Sinners therefore which be in so great and miserable need of help have much need of the great mercy of Almighty God. For the which Saint Paul sheweth the largeness of grace was given for the greatness of sin: *Ubi abundavit delictum, superabundavit et gratia:* "Whereas sin was abundant, grace was superabundant." But Almighty God will never have mercy on them that forsake His grace and turn themselves away from Him, but if[1] they will be turned again to Him by penance. For without doubt He is merciful and will exercise His

---

[1] unless.

mercy indeed upon them that will turn to Him by penance. For it is written in Ecclesiasticus: *Quam magna misericordia Domini et propitiatio illius convertentibus ad se:* "How great is the mercy and merciful doing of God to those that will turn them to Him." David therefore, after he had sinned and turned himself by penance unto God, asketh this petition, that our Lord of His goodness would vouchsafe to be turned again to him, delivering his soul from all perils. He fortifieth his reason by His mercy, saying: *Propter misericordiam tuam:* "Good Lord save me for Thy great mercy." Not only he allegeth His mercy to bind His reason, but also His wisdom; for because he is His creature and of His operation, therefore God of His wisdom should not suffer him to perish. It should seem that he was created of God but in vain and for nothing, without he might come to the end that he was made for. He was brought forth into this world by His creation, to the intent he should know God, and, that knowledge had, should love Him, and in that love he should always bear God in his remembrance and never cease in giving thanks to Him for His innumerable benefits. But these things cannot be done in Purgatory, and much less in Hell; for in Purgatory is so great sorrow for the innumerable pains, that the souls there may scant have remembrance of anything else save only those pains. Sith it is so that the sorrows of this world more vehemently occupieth the mind than doth the pleasures, and also the pleasures of this world (if they be great and over many) will not suffer the soul to remember itself; much less therefore it shall have any remembrance abiding in torments. For cause[1] also the pains of Purgatory be much more than the pains of this world, who may remember God as he ought to do, being in that painful place? Therefore the prophet saith: *Quoniam non est in morte qui memor sit tui:* "No creature being in Purgatory may have Thee in remembrance as he should." Then sith it is so that in Purgatory we cannot laud and praise God, how shall we do if we be in Hell?

[1] because.

Truly in that terrible place no creature shall neither love
God, neither laud Him. But alway they shall be inured
with continual hatred and blasphemings, crying out upon
Almighty God and despising His holy Name. This prophet for this cause addeth saying: *In inferno autem quis
confitebitur tibi?* "Blessed Lord, what creature shall
honour and worship Thee in Hell?" Thirdly, he fortifieth his reason by the rightwiseness[1] of God on this wise.
God is rightwise, wherefore He may not of right punish
twice for one and the same cause: an offence once punished, it is not right that the same be punished again.
The goodness of Almighty God giveth us time and space
to punish our own self by doing due penance for our
trespasses; and that done sufficiently, He is content so to
forgive us without any more punishment: which Saint
Paul witnessed saying: *Si nosmetipsos dijudicaremus non
utique dijudicaremur:* "If we give straight judgment
against ourself by doing due penance, Almighty God
shall never after judge us by His straight punishment."
The holy prophet sheweth what pain and punishment he
useth against himself, saying: *Laboravi in gemitu meo:*
"I have laboured in my weeping." The weeping heartily
for sins is of so great virtue and strength unto God that
for one weeping coming from the heart of a sinner, our
Lord forgiveth his trespass. *Nam in quacunque hora
peccator ingemuerit salvus erit:* "For whenever a sinner
weepeth and waileth heartily for his sins, he shall be
saved." Weeping doeth that thing in the soul which
rubbing and fretting doeth in the iron. Rubbing taketh
away rust and cankering from the iron. And weeping
putteth away from the soul the infection of sin. The
iron with rubbing anon will shine full bright. So the soul
with weeping is made fair and white. Weeping cometh
of the very sorrow from the heart, like as sin is caused
and cometh of the unlawful pleasures of the body. So
doth hearty weeping for sin expel sin, and is a sufficient
and just recompense for it. But here it is to be noted
that the prophet said not only he wept, but also he said:

[1] righteousness.

Laboravi in gemitu meo: " I have laboured in my weeping." What other thing is it to "labour in weeping,"
but as we might say, almost to be made weary with weeping? Therefore this prophet wailed and wept oftentimes
for his sins, in so much he thought in himself, for the
great labours in his weepings, almost for to have been
overcome; to the intent he might duly and sufficiently
punish his body in this life. Also he wept not only, but
also very sore and pitifully, for because he might wash
every sin in him with his bitter tears. In like wise as
we see by rusty and cankered pots, when they shall be
made clean, first they rub away the rust, and after that
wash it with water. So did this holy prophet, first by his
weeping scoured and made full clean his soul from the
rustiness and cankering of his foul sin, and after washed
it with his weeping tears. He made his promise not
only once or twice to do, but also every night to weep
and wail; he saith: *Lavabo per singulas noctes lectum
meum lacrimis meis:* " I shall every night wash my bed
with my weeping tears." And by this said bed is understand[1] the filthy voluptuousness of the body, wherein the
sinner walloweth and wrappeth himself like as a sow walloweth in the stinking gore-pit or in the puddle. If
thou wilt understand by the nights the darkness of sins,
then it is all one to wash every night thy bed and to weep
and wail the pleasure of thy body by the sorrowful remembrance of all thy sins one after another. It followeth
again in the same: *Stratum meum rigabo:* " I shall wash
my bed." By this bed is understand the heap and multitude of sins wherein all be heaped and gathered together
upon a rock.[2] Then if every oblectation[3] of sin shall be
done away by weeping tears, it may well be called a great
shower or a flood of them wherewith the heap of sins
shall be washed away. Fourthly he maketh his reason
by the great power of Almighty God: by this manner.
It seemeth[4] not so great majesty to exercise and prove
His strength upon a feeble and weak person; for then

---

[1] understood. [2] – *ruck*, a stack. [3] delight.
[4] beseemeth.

it should be as Job sayeth: *Contra folium quod vento rapitur potentiam ostenderet suam:* "He should shew and prove his strength against the leaf that with a little wind is wagged and blown down." It becometh not Him so to do which hath all power and is almighty, but rather that He defend and save them that be impotent and feeble; for of them that foolishly did tempt the goodness of Almighty God it is written: *Et salvavit eos propter nomen suum ut notam faceret potentiam suam:* "He saved them for His holy Name that His power might be known." On this wise without doubt the power of Almighty God is shewed to His great honour and glory. What praise were it to a giant to fight against a gnat, or how should his strength be known although He have the better of the gnat? Should He not be dispraised for that victory? Great laud and praise is in wild beasts lacking reason, that they will forgive and not venge themselves upon other weaker beasts that acknowledgeth their feebleness and bow down to them. They abstain from their cruelty and malice. *Parcere prostratis vult nobilis ira leonis:* "The lion is so noble that in his anger he will not hurt the beast that falleth down and meeketh[1] himself unto him." Shall not therefore God, to Whom is ascribed all goodness and praise that may be in any creature, be meek and gentle? And shall He not be patient and spare weak and feeble creatures, meeking themself and owning their own infirmity? Yes, doubtless; for the more that a man is endued with the virtue of strength, the more meek and gentle shall he be. Therefore Almighty God, that is most mighty of all, must needs be most gentle and meek. The prophet therefore sheweth his feebleness, willing thereby to move the goodness of God to mercy and pity. *Turbatus est a furore oculus meus.* He saith, "Good Lord, the eye of my soul is troubled and feared of thine infinite punishment." In another place he saith: *Quis novit potestatem irae tuae: aut prae timore iram tuam dinumerare?* "Blessed Lord, who may know the greatness of Thy punishment, or for

[1] humbleth.

fear dare take upon him to measure it?" He therefore, considering in himself the great punishment of Almighty God, and in manner as he would measure it, perceiveth well that it is much. It is no marvel then though he fear, also quake for fear and always be in dread of the punishment of God or ever[1] it fall upon him. Beholding also with the eye of his soul the cruelty of his infinite pain (which, as we said before, cannot be mitigate), how may he be but sore troubled both in soul and body? Therefore with great fear and dread prostrate before Almighty God he saith: *Turbatus est a furore oculus meus:* " Good Lord, the eye of my soul is sore troubled for fear of Thine everlasting punishment; and not only, Blessed Saviour, do I suffer this, but also I am oft overcome of mine enemies, the flesh, the world, and the devils, that utterly my strength be gone. I am brought to nought and wax feeble and old, not able of mine own self to stand in their hands."[2] *Inveteravi inter omnes inimicos meos:* " I am old and unwieldy, having no strength to withstand mine enemies." The whole effect of this fourth reason is this. Since it is so that this prophet is in so great feebleness and submitting himself all whole to God, He of His great power may not be but merciful to him.

The third part of this Psalm is yet behind, wherein the prophet trusting verily of forgiveness joyeth in himself with a bold and hardy spirit. The virtue and strength of the grace of God is marvellous, that where it once pierceth and entereth into the soul of any creature, it maketh him bold and to hope well, in so much that he dare make battle afresh against his enemies. Take heed and behold the sudden change of this prophet, caused by the goodness of God; where but late he was vexed and troubled with fear and dread, nevertheless now being comforted by the grace of Almighty God, he hath audacity to despise his enemies and command them to go away from him. He saith: *Discedite a me omnes qui operamini iniquitatem:* " All ye that be the doers of wickedness, I command you, go from me." Truly the

---

[1] ere.   [2] against them.

C

doers of wickedness be they which busieth themselves
and be about to cause sins to be done, like as the damned
spirits were first, by whose enticement sin entered first
into man's soul. Of this disposition be the wicked and
malicious devils which never go about other thing but
that they may craftily deceive with their frauds and bring
men's souls into the snares of sin. Therefore this prophet saith unto them: *Discedite a me omnes qui operamini iniquitatem:* "Go from me all ye that be the doers
of wickedness." He sheweth the reason why they ought
to go from him, for because he belongeth not to them.
As long as he was the servant of sin, so long was he
under the power of Satan and his ministers. But now
since that by true penance he hath turned himself unto
Almighty God and hath utterly cast away and forsaken
his sins, he is clean delivered from the power of the
devils. But what is the cause of this? It followeth:
Quoniam exaudivit Dominus vocem fletus mei: "For our
Lord of His goodness hath heard the voice of my weeping." Take heed how great the virtue is of weeping
tears, that when they be shed from the heart of a true
penitent, anon they ascend unto the high throne of Almighty God, and also they be heard in His ear. They be
not heard only, but also they be graciously heard. The
petition asked by them is granted, and taken into the
bosom of the high majesty of God. And for that cause
he saith: *Quoniam exaudivit Dominus vocem fletus mei.
Exaudivit Dominus deprecationem meam: Dominus ora-
tionem meam suscepit:* "Our Lord hath heard the voice
of my weeping. Our Lord hath heard my prayer, and
also acceptably taken up my petition." Now here give
heed with how great inward joy this prophet advanceth
himself when he doubleth and so oft rehearseth that
he is graciously heard of Almighty God. Truly the joy
that a true penitent hath is great when he understandeth
and knoweth himself to be at liberty from the servitude
and danger of sin. The prophet is joyful and glad that
he is clean delivered from the power of his adversaries,
and maketh imprecation against them that they for their
malice may be shamed and greatly troubled. Certainly

the devils ought to be ashamed, and not unworthy[1] when they so vehemently do against Almighty God their Maker. They be not ashamed to draw and induce unto their service those persons which studieth gladly to serve Almighty God, and of this they ought to be more ashamed than the same persons which they think verily be surely in their possession and as creatures forsaken of our Lord God. Nevertheless as soon as they be penitent and willing to forsake their sins, they be utterly delivered from their power; and also they dare no more meddle with them, for the which they be sore vexed and troubled, seeing their prey, whether they will or will not, to be taken away from them. Certainly then they gnash with their teeth, they wail, they be full of wrath and wax wood.[2] And that they may oft be vexed on this wise, the prophet maketh this imprecation: *Erubescant et conturbentur vehementer omnes inimici mei*. This imprecation is good and rightwise. For why? Great honour by it is given to Almighty God, great help and succour unto them that be penitent, great joy to them that be rightwise of overcoming their enemies, and marvellous great confusion unto the devils. Wherefore the prophet again maketh his imprecation, desiring that sinners may be turned to God, and forsake their sinful life, and by that the devils may be more and more ashamed. *Convertantur et erubescant:* " Blessed Lord, give sinners that grace they may be turned to the great shame and confusion of the devils." *Valde velociter:* " And grant that it may be done shortly."

THE SECOND PENITENTIAL PSALM.

BEATI QUORUM.

PSALM xxxi

THIS Psalm, of a good congruence and not unworthy,[3] is called a Penitential Psalm because penance is so diligently treated and spoken of in it. First the prophet praiseth them whose sins be utterly done away by

[1] undeservedly. [2] mad. [3] properly and not undeservedly.

penance. Again he sheweth the wretchedness of those that forsake penance. Also he sheweth the occasion and manner of contrition, confession, and satisfaction, which be the three parts of penance. First he praiseth greatly the virtue of contrition, namely whereas[1] there is a full purpose of confession. He teacheth also the necessity of it. He sheweth also the impediments of it, and remedies for the same. He comforteth and lifteth up them that be weak in soul. He calleth again those that be out of the right way to come to bliss, and in manner threateneth them. He promiseth damnation to them that refuseth penance; to them that doeth it, forgiveness; to them that go forward and profit in it, joy. And last he promiseth eternal glory to those that be perfect. This holy prophet goeth shortly on all these in the same orders as we have rehearsed to you.

It is great praise to them whose sins be done away by penance to be called blessed. And truly there is no other thing else in this world that may so speedfully cause any creature to be blessed, as purging of sin by penance. For bodily health, fairness or beauty, strength, agility or activeness, honours, riches, and other such pleasures worldly, rather bring a man out of the right and true way of beatitude; which daily we may behold and perceive in many, that, if they had wanted[2] these pleasures, should more diligently have holden themselves in the path that bringeth and leadeth us unto the blessed life. No creature liveth that never did amiss. For as Saint James saith: *In multis offendimus omnes:* "We all have offended in many causes." He that hath offendeth hath erred and gone out of the right way. And the coming again into the right way is only made open and shewed to him by penance. Therefore only they that be penitent are blessed; for they and none other take their journey into the heavenly country where is very blessedness. Now in this life by true faith and hope; and after, in very deed.

But since penance hath three divers parts, that is to say, contrition, confession, and satisfaction, the more

---

[1] where.   [2] been without.

diligently that any creature exerciseth himself in every one of them, the more near he is unto the eternal bliss; for by those three, like as by so many instruments, we make a perfect rasing[1] and cleansing of the soul from sins. When we be about to rase and do away any manner writing, we first scrape the paper; and by that rasure or scraping, somewhat is taken away of the letters, and there is a deformity of the very perfect knowledge, that the letters may not be perceived and discerned but darkly. If we rase it again, the letters shall be utterly done away and put out of knowledge; and if we do so the third time, then shall nothing of the least letter be seen, but as clean as ever it was. So in like manner we shall remember to be done in our souls for doing away of our sins by the three parts of penance. By the virtue of contrition our sins be forgiven; by confession they be forgotten; but by satisfaction they be so clean done away that no sign or token remaineth in any condition of them, but as clean as ever we were. Albeit after contrition and confession sin be done away, yet a duty remaineth in the soul that needs must be paid and performed by suffering pain. For although by contrition and confession the pain eternal that we should have suffered be done away, nevertheless there abideth in the soul a certain taxation or duty which without doubt must needs be contented and satisfied either here in this life by temporal pain or else after this life in Purgatory. But whereas any creature have[2] made due satisfaction in this life, he never after shall suffer more pain; and also he is clean out of debt, and nothing after that shall ever be claimed of him. Wherefore the prophet saith: *Beati quorum remissæ sunt iniquitates:* "Blessed be they whose sins be forgiven." Behold first the remission of sin by contrition. *Et quorum tecta sunt peccata:* "Blessed be they whose sins be hid and put out of knowledge"; which is done by confession. *Beatus vir cui non imputavit Dominus peccatum:* "Blessed is he to whom our Lord hath not imputed or laid any sin to his charge." Behold the third time, the whole and perfect doing away of sin by

---

[1] scraping.   [2] whenever any creature shall have.

satisfaction. Many there be that wail and be contrite and also confess their sins, but scant one among a thousand can be found that doeth due satisfaction. Therefore whereas before the prophet shewed in the plural number signifying that many were blessed whose sins be forgiven, covered and put out of knowledge, now he speaketh in the singular number signifying that few be which do due satisfaction. *Beatus vir cui non imputavit Dominus peccatum:* " Blessed is that creature unto whom our Lord hath imputed no sin." The mercy and goodness of Almighty God shewed upon sinners is marvellous great ; which, the more that they call unto their own mind and express their own trespasses, so much the more He forgetteth and putteth them out of His mind ; and the more diligently they shew them without gloss or deceit, to the intent they may be openly known by confession, the more busily He covereth and putteth them out of knowledge ; and last, the more that they think and ascribe their offences to their own great unkindness, punishing themselves for their errors, so much less He layeth any trespass to their charge, but utterly He taketh away their sin and leaveth nothing of it behind. We be shewed and warned that it is not only enough to be contrite and confessed for our offences, but also we must be busy in doing good works to make satisfaction for them. For if we be negligent in this third part of penance, which is satisfaction, it is to be feared lest in us be some manner privy guile or fault, whereby we be deceived. Like as we see, if a tree hath brought forth buds and flowers, and after that bringeth forth no fruit, we think verily that some default is within the tree which is cause thereof. Even so in man's soul which first hath brought forth the bud of contrition, and after the flower, confession, if at the last it bring not forth the good works of satisfaction, it is to be dreaded lest any privy guile or deceit remain still in the soul ; that is to say, it is not very contrite and truly confessed : there lacketh very contrition and true confession. That person which hath all three parts of penance, contrition, confession, and satisfaction, is never beguiled, but doubtless he goeth in the right path that leadeth the way unto everlasting bliss. Therefore the prophet addeth, saying: *Nec est in spiritu eius dolus.* He that hath done his duty and constrained himself so busily and so many times to make satisfaction for his offences that our Lord in any condition shall impute no trespass or fault unto him, truly " in his soul is no deceit nor guile " either of untrue contrition or feigned confession. In this life contrition may soon be had by the grace of God with a little sorrow. Also the sacrament of absolution is a great help unto them that hath made their whole confession. For it is said of Almighty God to them that hath power for to hear confession: *Quorum remiseritis peccata remittuntur eis.* The injunction of a good deed (in the way of satisfaction) of[1] a man's own ghostly father hath great virtue; but if it be taken with a good will, it is of much more efficacy and strength, for it is written: *Melior est obedientia quam stultorum victimæ:* "Obedience is better than foolish sacrifice." Now if we refuse and take no heed to that thing whereof the prophet admonisheth us, we be greatly to be blamed; and not without a cause, since only by that way we must come to eternal bliss. For if we will not study and be about[2] to purge our souls by these means, by the three parts of penance afore rehearsed, we take not the way to bliss but unto misery and wretchedness. Truly as in Heaven, where is all goodness and pleasure without end, is very bliss; so in Hell, whereas is all evil and no pleasure, is most wretchedness: to the which misery we be brought by our sin. And contrariwise we be brought unto bliss by purging of our sins. Moreover if the filthiness of sin be once conceived in the soul, and long continue there by unhappy custom, it maketh foul and infecteth it more and more; as we see by urine or any other stinking liquor put in a vessel, the longer it be kept in the same, so much more it maketh foul the vessel and corrupteth it. Another example. As we see a boil or botch full of matter and filth, the more and the longer it be hid, the more groweth the corruption and venomous infection of it, and also pierceth to the bones and cor-

---

[1] by.   [2] bestir ourselves.

rupteth them. In like wise the longer that sins be kept close in the souls, the more feeble they be made and the more contagiously corrupt. Also they infect the strong parts of the soul, the virtues of the soul, and bringeth them out of custom of doing good works. The prophet, following the said similitude, addeth saying: *Quoniam tacui, inveteraverunt ossa mea:* "Because I purged not my soul by contrition of my sins, but privily did hold my peace and kept them within me, therefore the virtues of it be consumed by long continuance in the filthiness of sin." *Dum clamarem tota die:* "And this was done notwithstanding I cried out and made my vaunt all day." How may this be? The prophet before saith he held his peace, and now he sheweth that he cried all day. Peradventure he kept secret one thing and shewed another. Truly if we ourselves have done anything that is good, anon we be glad to shew it openly to the knowledge of every man. And contrariwise if we have done an evil deed or anything amiss, we do as much as we can possibly to hide it. If also we do anything that is praiseworthy, we shew it and in manner cry it out over all; and if we do shrewdly,[1] we hide it, we hold our peace, and keep it secret. So peradventure the prophet shewed his own lauds and praises and kept secret his offences, whereof he should accuse himself. For that cause he said: *Quoniam tacui, inveteraverunt ossa mea dum clamarem tota die:* "Because I did hold my peace and would not accuse my defaults, and also shewed openly and made my vaunt of all my well-doings and praises, therefore the virtues of my soul were long discontinued and brought out of use." The occasion that causeth and bringeth us to wretchedness is, if we shew not and accuse ourself of all our sins by confession, but keep them secret. But by what occasion be we wrought and led into the right way of very bliss? The wise man saith: *Timor Domini expellit peccatum:* "The dread of God putteth away sin." Wherefore the dread of God is the beginning of putting away of sin. Let us call to remembrance the saying of Saint Paul to the Romans, where he treateth them that

[1] evilly.

lie continually in sin and will do no penance: *Secundum duritiam tuam et cor impœnitens thesaurizas tibi iram in die iræ*. That is to say, " We provoke the goodness of Almighty God to punish us because of our sturdiness, and will not turn to Him by doing penance, and in manner we give Him occasion to shew vengeance and destroy us both body and soul." For truly over our heads hangeth a sword, ever moving and ready, by the power of God; whose stroke, when it shall come, shall be so much more grievous that we so long by our great and manifold unkindness have called Almighty God and provoked Him to more displeasure. Which would God we all were in mind to remember. For the prophet beareth witness that he took occasion to forsake his sin and turn himself to our blessed and merciful Lord God by the fear of His great punishment, saying: *Quoniam die ac nocte gravata est super me manus tua, conversus sum*. " Good Lord, I am turned to Thee." For why? " The fear of Thy great punishment troubleth me both day and night and at all times." David understood that Almighty God was displeased with him, by the words spoken of the prophet Nathan, saying: *Non recedet de domo tua gladius eo quod despexeris me:* " I shall punish thee and thy lineage because thou despised Me." By the which words the heart of David had as sore a stroke, when he remembered his sin, as it had been pierced through with the sharpest thorn that might be. For doubtless the remembrance of sin pricketh and teareth the conscience of a penitent creature even as sore as the thorn doth that is sticked fast in a man's body. This holy prophet by the sore and bitter pricking of his conscience was made so sorrowful and so full of wretchedness, that he is fain to turn to Almighty God. Also he is come again to himself, whereas before he was beside himself. Every sinner not willing to forsake his sin is beside himself. For our Saviour said: *Ubi est thesaurus tuus, ibi est et cor tuum:* " Where thy treasure is, there is thine heart." And Saint Austin saith: *Verius est ibi animus ubi amat quam ubi animat:* " The mind of a man is more there where it loveth than it is upon himself." David therefore, in love

with Bersabee, had more mind on her than on himself.
Nevertheless when his conscience by the remembrance of
his sin was pricked, like as I might be thrust through
with a thorn, and he coming again to himself, fearing
and sorrowing, he turned unto God and forsook his sin.
He saith: *Conversus sum in ærumna mea dum configitur
spina:* "Good Lord, when my conscience was sore pricked
by the remembrance of mine own wretchedness I turned
myself to Thee." There be two things, therefore, which
be the very cause that we turn ourselves unto Almighty
God: one is when we call to mind His fearful and
grievous punishment; the other is the sorrow in our heart
when we remember the multitude of our sins, whereby
our best and most meek Lord God is greatly discontented
with us. The fear of the punishment of God is cause
of sorrow for sin, and whosoever is in the calamity of
this great fear and sorrow, he turneth himself unto Almighty God without doubt; and the moving of the soul
first caused of fear, and after of sorrow, referred unto
God, is called contrition, which is the first part of
penance.

After that followeth the second part, which we said
is confession. It is not enough for a penitent to be contrite for his sins, but also he must shew them all unto a
priest, his ghostly father, when he hath convenient time
and place so to do. For as we said before, if we ourselves hide and cover our sins, Almighty God shall un-
cover them. And if we again make open and shew them,
He shall hide and put them out of knowledge. David
therefore, when by the remembrance of his sins he was
pricked in his conscience, like as he had been thrust
through the heart with a thorn, turned himself unto Almighty God with all his heart, and confessed his sin to
the prophet of God, and coming to him, said: *Peccavi
Domino:* "I have offended my Lord God." And we in
like manner which be compunct and grudge in our conscience when we remember the great multitude of our
sins whereby we have greatly displeased Almighty God,
let us accuse ourselves and shew our sins by a true and
holy confession, that everyone of us may say with the

prophet this that followeth: *Delictum meum cognitum tibi jeci:* "Good Lord, I myself have acknowledged and made open my trespass unto Thee."

And thirdly we shall be about[1] ever, as much as we may, to make amends for our offences by the works of satisfaction, that our sins in any condition be not laid to our charge at any time. For although contrition causeth forgiveness of sin, and confession covereth and putteth it out of knowledge, nevertheless satisfaction doth rase and expel it so clean away that no sign can ever after be spied of it. In the old law there were certain sacrifices, certain oblations and certain ceremonies assigned according to the diversities of sins, whereby amends should be made for them. Notwithstanding, David, for fear and shame that his offences should be known unto the people, would not use any of those ceremonies. I fear me, many nowadays be of that condition: they will not weep, they will not sorrow, they will not abstain from their old customs and uses, lest it should be thought that they had done amiss. Dear brethren, let not us do so; let us appear and shew ourself even as we be. Truly all we be sinners, for if we say no sin is in us, we condemn ourself and say not truth: therefore let us shew ourself as sinners. And since it is convenient and according for sinners to wail, to weep, to fast, and to abstain from the voluptuous pleasures of their bodies, we must either weep and wail in this life with profitable weeping tears wherewith the soul is washed and made clean from sin, else shall we wail and weep after this life with unprofitable tears which intolerably shall scald and burn our bodies, and that without end. Let us therefore follow the penance of Mary Magdalene and do thereafter. Let not worldly shame fear[2] us to weep for our sins; let no manner shamefastness cause us to do the contrary, but that we may wail at any time and take sharp pain on us, which is due for sin, to the intent we may all say with the prophet (which followeth): *Et injustitiam meam non abscondi:* "Good Lord I have acknowledged mine unrightwiseness unto Thee. I have not kept it

---

[1] busy.   [2] make us afraid.

secret." Furthermore, it may so be that a person wail
and be very contrite for his offences, albeit he may not
have an able[1] and convenient ghostly father when he
would. It may also fortune a man to be sorry for his sin
and to be confessed of the same, yet peradventure
the stroke of death, which is importune and cannot be
avoided, may be so nigh him that he can have no time
and space for to make satisfaction for his offences. For
this cause, lest that any creature should despair and have
any mistrust in the great mercy of God, the holy prophet
sheweth how great the virtue is of contrition with a full
purpose of confession. Only[2] contrition with a full purpose of confession taketh away the guilt of sin. So that
whosoever is contrite and purposing to be confessed if
he might, and fall not again into sin, shall never be
damned. Nevertheless, I cannot tell if any bond abide
in the soul (after the sin be taken away), of any pain
taxed by the rightwiseness of God due for sin; which
pain either must be satisfied and done away in this life
by the works of satisfaction, or else in Purgatory by
suffering of sharp and grievous pains there. But, notwithstanding, as we said before, the sin is done away
by contrition with a full purpose of confession. This
holy prophet saith: *Dixi confitebor adversum me injustitiam meam Domino: et tu remisisti impietatem peccati
mei:* " I have had a full purpose to confess my own unrightwiseness, mine own trespass against myself unto my
Lord God, and Thou good Lord hast forgiven my sin."
Behold, his sin is forgiven because he purposed to be
truly confessed: many things being required to a true
and whole confession. First that the penitent confess
all his sins together and leave none behind, wherefore he
saith: *Confitebor:* " I shall acknowledge together all my
sins," not accusing his fate or destiny, nor any constella-
tion, neither the devil or any other thing, but only his
own self; therefore he saith: *Adversum me:* " I shall
make confession against myself and none other." But
what shall he confess? Truly his own errors in breaking the commandment of God, how oft he hath declined

---

[1] qualified.   [2] mere.

unrightfully and contrary to His law. He shall not confess another man's trespass, but only his own; therefore
it followeth: *Injustitiam meam:* " I shall confess mine
own fault, mine own sin, mine own unrightwiseness." And
to whom shall he acknowledge himself guilty, and to
what intent? *Domino.* Verily to our Lord God, and to
His honour, to the confusion of the devil, and also to re-
cover his own soul's health. Whosoever in this wise have
a full purpose to shew his sin by confession with sorrow
and penance of contrition for the same, if case be death
come upon him immediately, yet should he never suffer
eternal damnation. But verily confession, shewing of sin,
busy doing of good works for satisfaction, shall never
be sufficient without some sorrow and penance for the
same. For without doubt penance and contrition is so
necessary unto these that will be saved that without them
(if they have sinned) their sin cannot be forgiven. And
I pray you, who liveth that never sinned? *Neque enim
est homo qui non peccat.* Scripture saith none. Since
therefore every man and woman be sinners, we all have
need of contrition, for without it we shall never come to
Heaven. Peter offended grievously in denying his Master, Christ. Paul in pursuing His Church. Mary Magdalene sinned grievously in misusing the pleasures of her
body; and many other without number were sinners, almost so many as now be saints in Heaven. There is no
saint in Heaven (a few excepted) but, ere they came there,
had need some time to ask of Almighty God the gift of
contrition. The prophet saith: *Pro hac orabit ad te omnis sanctus in tempore opportuno:* " Good Lord, every
creature that trusteth to be saved shall pray to Thee for
contrition in a convenient time." Opportunity is to be
inquired and looked for in everything to be done; and
it is called the office of a wise man to use it as it should
be, when it cometh. Of a truth sometimes the soul is
marvellously much holden down, covered and hid with
so many divers pleasures of worldly flattering, that it
may not rise up and help itself. When also it is called
unto the own country, which is Heaven, it will not hear;
it forsaketh the own health when it is offered and prof-

fered. Why? For then is none opportunity, no con-
veniency, or no convenient time. Truly no impediment
earthy doth more stiffly and strongly withstand very
contrition, than doth over-many worldly pleasures,
which be shrewd and noisome to the soul.

In the beginning of the world Almighty God
made Paradise a place of honest pleasure. And from
that place issueth out a flood divided into four
parts, signifying the four capital virtues, Rightwiseness,
Temperance, Prudence, and Strength, wherewith the
whole soul might be washed and made pleasant, like
as with so many floods. But on the contrary wise,
the devil hath conceived and made another manner
Paradise of bodily and sensual pleasures. And from
thence cometh out other four floods, very contrary unto
the other: that is to say, the flood of Covetousness
contrary to Justice, the flood of Gluttony against Temperance, the flood of Pride against Prudence, and the
flood of Lechery against Strength. Whosoever be
drowned in any of these floods, it is hard for them to be
turned to God by true contrition: the raging of them
is so great and overflowing. For this cause the prophet saith: *Verumtamen in diluvio aquarum multarum
ad eum non approximabunt:* "They that have all the pleasures of this world, and in manner be drowned in them,
shall not draw nigh Almighty God for their salvation."
But what remedy for us that be amongst all these floods?
Whither shall we flee? Truly God is only the remedy
and refuge, without Whose help no man may scape them
without drowning. Many there hath been in time past
that hath scaped the peril and danger of these floods by
the help of God right well. Abraham and Job were men
of great riches and worldly substance; nevertheless it was
nothing noisome[1] to them. For why? They were holy
and perfect men for all that; although they were rich,
yet they had no covetous mind nor covetous desire of
worldly substance; and always content, whatsoever God
sent unto them either prosperity or adversity. They did
not set their mind on gold or riches. It may be spoken

---

[1] hurtful.

of them both as the Wise Man said: *Beatus vir qui post aurum non abiit:* "Blessed is that creature which setteth not his mind upon gold or riches." Always when they were most in the pleasures of the world, they lift up their minds unto Almighty God, Which held them up and was their safeguard from drowning. Also more there was that escaped, by the help of God, the danger of the other floods, Lechery and Gluttony. Edward,[1] sometime king of England, lived with his well-beloved wife: notwithstanding, he was chaste and kept his virginity for God's sake; and besides that, being king, he despised both honours and riches. Louis,[2] sometime king of France, led his life in like manner, with many other innumerable. When they knew and perceived well the peril and danger that might fall by the possession of worldly riches, they fled from them and called for help to Almighty God, saying *Salvum me fac, Domine, quoniam intraverunt aquæ usque ad animam meam:* "Good Lord save me, for the floods of the world trouble me on every side both in body and in soul." Let us therefore, when we perceive the danger of this worldly and transitory riches, call unto Almighty God for help, and say as the prophet said, this (which followeth in this Psalm) :*Tu es refugium meum a tribulatione quæ circumdedit me:* "Lord, Thou only art my help and refuge in this tribulation of worldly temptation and pleasures which ravenously hath gone round about to catch me." This flood of worldly covetousness rageth and floweth on every side and is about to overwhelm us. Saint John saith *Omne enim quod est in mundo aut est concupiscentia carnis aut concupiscentia oculorum aut superbia vitæ:* "All things that is of this world, either it is the desire of the flesh, either the concupiscence of the sight, or else proud living." Take heed, he saith, "all that is in this world"; therefore it must follow that it is so in every part of the world. Either we be moved and stirred to lusty pleasures and likings in meat and drink and clothing with such other which nourisheth the flesh, and maketh it prone and ready to gluttony and lechery; else we be moved to

---

[1] the Confessor.   [2] Saint Louis.

have riches and possessions which feedeth the sight, and
by the sight we be induced to unlawful desires that is
covetous; either we be moved to have honours and great
dignities, or else worldly praising which bringeth in
pride.   In this wise these floods take their course round
about throughout the world; they spare almost none, that
no place of sure help and refuge can be had whereunto
we may flee, but only Almighty God.   Each one of us,
willing to flee unto our Lord God, may say with the prophet *Exultatio mea, erue me a circumdantibus me:* "O
my Lord God, my joy and my only succour, deliver me
from these troublesome floods of this world which go
round about me."   I cannot escape them without Thy
help.

But now let us a while give heed what comfort and
consolation we shall take by doing penance.   Three
things there be that bindeth us needs[1] to do penance.
First the profound consideration of the greatness of our
sin.   The second, open shewing of the same to a priest
by confession.   And the third, the diligent exercising
of good works.

Understanding is necessary to be had for the first,
which must search profoundly for the grievousness of
every sin.   For the second, instruction and learning is
necessary, whereby we may judge and descry the diversity
of one sin from another; and so to shew every one of
them in confession with all their circumstances.   To the
third the grace of God is in especial necessary, wherewith
they be plentifully infused and endued on whom our merciful Lord looketh with the eyes of His mercy and grace.
From the eyes of Almighty God, which may be called His
grace, shineth forth a marvellous brightness like as the
beam that cometh from the sun.   And that light of grace
stirreth and setteth forward the soul to bring forth the
fruit of good works, even as the light of the sun causeth
herbs to grow and trees to bring forth fruit.   Therefore
if we that be set amongst the perilous floods of these
worldly pleasures will lift up our minds to God, not set-
ting our felicity on them, busily asking His help, He shall

[1] necessarily.

comfort us. According to the words of the prophet Our
Lord shall say unto us *Intellectum tibi dabo:* " I shall
give thee understanding," which is necessary to consider
profoundly our sins. That is for the first. For the
second, which is confession, He shall say *Instruam te:* " I
shall give thee learning, whereby thou shalt discern of
every sin." For the third, that is satisfaction, He shall
say *In via hac qua gradieris firmabo super te oculos meos:*
" I shall guide and direct thee from thine enemies with
My grace and mercy, ever to have continuance in doing
good works." O marvellous meekness of Almighty God
shewed unto sinners when they flee unto Him, which is
so ready to comfort and grant them help, whereby they
may be sure to escape from overflowing and drowning
in these floods of the transitory pleasures of this world !
Which meekness our prophet remembering, calleth and
exhorteth every creature to do penance. And whereas
before he hath shewed and spoken much of it, first, that
they which be penitent are blessed, they that refuse
penance be wretched ; which also be the causes of doing
penance; how many parts there be of it; what strength
penance is of ; how much it is necessary ; the impediments
of the same ; what remedy for the impediments ; and how
ready Almighty God is at hand to help us: now, after
the short expressing of these, he is about to lift up the
minds of sinners to the exercising and using of it. Two
kinds there be of sinners which refuse to do penance.
One is of them that follow their own pleasure in everything, and as wild beasts that never were bridled, use
themselves in the unlawful desire of the flesh, like unto a
horse. The other is of them that hath been long brought
up, peradventure till they come to age, in the ungracious
custom of sin. And because they have been of old time
so long in the use of the same, they will continue in it still,
and in no wise go out of that way. They be like to a
mule. Man that was created in great honour, (and among
all creatures living none but he had their face set straight
to look up into Heaven), endued also with reason and free
will, formed and made like unto the image of Almighty
God, ordained by His Maker to be above all other crea-

D

tures of the world, and they also to be at his commandment—alas that he on this wise hath deformed and
changed himself by sin unto an unreasonable beast, also
forgetting Almighty God His Maker, hath made himself
like to a horse and a mule, forsaking wholesome penance
offered to him by our Lord God, whereby he might have
been reformed and brought again into his first state and
honour! The prophet therefore, willing to excite and
raise up the minds of sinners that be overcome with this
unhappy and miserable blindness, speaketh unto them
with these words *Nolite fieri sicut equus et mulus, quibus
non est intellectus:* " Be not in will to be made like to a
horse and a mule, following your own sensual pleasure
and appetite, in whom is none understanding." And,
fearing lest but few shall hear him, he turneth his sayings
to God. Truly our merciful Lord oftentimes enticeth by
His benefits many sinners to penance. Matthew, which
was a toll-gatherer, anon as he was called of God, forsook that life and followed Christ. Mary Magdalene
drawn by very love unto our Blessed Lord wept at His
feet. Our Lord looked meekly and mercifully upon
Peter, albeit Peter denied him thrice before he nevertheless shamed in himself and wept bitterly. Peradventure
when St. Anthony heard read in the Gospel at that time:
Qui reliquerit patrem et matrem, &c. (" Whosoever forsaketh their father and mother, sister and brother, and
the possessions of this world for the love of God shall be
rewarded a hundred times more for it, which is everlasting life ") he then forsook all and went into wilderness
and there lived. All these were sweetly called to penance,
and many more without number. Namely a certain priest
of whom speaketh the noble doctor Parisiense[1] was singularly called and provoked to be penitent. This priest
had many great gifts of God: notwithstanding, he every
day sinned more and more, and heaped sin upon sin. God
Almighty for all that left him not so, but still endued him
with new benefits, that at the last by consent of all the
people he was chosen and made a bishop. Then when he
perceived the goodness and meekness of Almighty God,

---

[1] William of Auvergne, Bp. of Paris, † 1248.

and remembered also how unkind he had been of long continuance to his Maker, he said: " O Blessed Lord, Thou hast overcome me. Thou hast utterly bound me by Thy grace and manifold benefits to be Thy servant; from henceforth I shall never go from Thee." And which one of us may say but that he hath been called to penance by the benefits of our Lord God? Let us all consider the merciful gifts that God hath given unto us. And hear the saying of St. Paul which asketh this question *An ignoras quoniam benignitas Dei ad pœnitentiam te invitat?* " Dost thou not know that the goodness of Almighty God calleth thee to penance?" If we will not be brought to penance by these fair means, by the great and manifold gifts of God, let us at the least fear His great and many grievous punishments; for sometimes Almighty God constraineth those obstinate sinners that will not be turned with fair means, by His punishments; and with them He dealeth mercifully to chastise and punish them in this life. For the which the prophet crieth upon Him to bring those that be so obdurate and sturdy, and in no wise will leave their unhappy custom of sin, but make themselves in condition like a wild horse or an ass, and to compel them by His punishment to do penance, saying: *In camo et freno maxillas eorum constringe qui non approximant ad te:* " Blessed Lord, constrain those sinners with Thy punishments, less and more, in this life, which will not come and draw nigh to Thee by penance." The great punishments in this life may be called the censures of the Church, as the great curse,[1] with other,[2] or temporal death. The less punishments may be called other temporal pains, as loss of worldly goods, sickness, with other. It is better for a sinner to suffer tribulation and punishment in this life, whereby he may get profit and be rewarded, than to be eternally tormented in Hell: for all the punishment there, be it ever so sharp and grievous, shall not profit. St. Augustine saith *Hic ure, hic seca:* " Good Lord, punish me in this life." Since so good and so holy a man desired of God to be sharply punished in this life, rather than after this life, to the

---

[1] among others.   [2] *i.e.*, major excommunication.

intent he might be able to have the everlasting kingdom of Heaven, what shall these obstinate sinners do that never would be turned by the great benefits of God? It had been far better for them to have suffered the greatest punishment that might be, in this life. For they shall be drawn down of the cruel tormentors, the devils, into the deep pit of Hell, there to be crucified eternally; where shall be weeping, wailing and gnashing of teeth; where also the worm of their conscience shall never die, and that fire shall never be quenched; where also part of their pain shall be in a pit full of burning liquor, and in fire and brimstone flaming continually. David saith *Multa flagella peccatoris:* "Many divers and grievous punishments be for the obstinate and hard-hearted sinner that never will be penitent." But whosoever in this life will do penance, were he never so great a sinner before, (if he despair not of forgiveness) Almighty God shall be merciful, and forgive him. For, as St. Augustine saith: "If all the sins of the world were compared to the mercy of God, they be in comparison no more to it than is a spark of fire in the great sea." And I dare well say to the sinner, be he never so wicked in his living, if at any time in this life he will be penitent for it and desire forgiveness and mercy of Almighty God, He of His great goodness will sooner forgive him than all the water in the sea can quench one spark of fire, if it were cast upon it; for when the sinner is very penitent, nothing remaineth in the soul that may withstand the infinite mercy of Almighty God, which standeth round about ready on every side. The prophet sheweth the same by these words following *Sperantem autem in Domino misericordia circumdabit:* "The mercy of God shall be ready round about on every side to defend the sinner that trusteth in Him and will do penance for his sins." Many there be which think great pleasure in sin and worldly pleasures. Truly those wretches be beguiled: it is not as they think. Doubtless they that be truly penitent have more felicity and pleasure in God and godly things, far in comparison above all worldly pleasures. For the more noble and better that the inward knowledge in judging or discerning is, (which may be called the virtue of perceiving or taking.) and the more excellent the thing be which is judged, the greater and goodlier pleasure must needs be felt inwardly when the thing is tasted, the nearer that the one be set and applied to the other. Example: the more perfect that a man's taste be, the greater pleasure shall he feel inwardly in tasting of that thing which hath a very pleasant savour, the more nigh that it be joined and put to the tongue. Then thus, since that the virtue and capacity of our soul is far better and more perfect than is the virtue of all our other knowledges, and also of all living creatures beside, and hath Almighty God and godly things the more nigh unto it the clearer that it be purged by due penance; it must needs follow that the penitent hath more sweet joy and gladness inwardly in his soul than any other creature living may have in all the pleasures of this world. When two things be compared together, the most sure knowledge of their diversity shall be had, of one that knoweth both and so to stand to his judgment. And doubtless many hath had in experience the pleasures of this world, and afterwards hath forsaken them and followed the way of bitter and sharp penance. Ask of them whether they have been more glad inwardly in the penitent life or in the temporal, without doubt they will answer, "in the penitent life, in the life of contemplation." I think there be no man but some time hath had the experience of the joy and pleasure that is in the soul after true confession and due penance for sin. If the first part of penance maketh the soul glad, how joyful shall it be when it is made clean throughout by all the parts of penance and nothing is left behind unpurged! Therefore the prophet saith *Lætamini in Domino et exultate justi: et gloriamini omnes recti corde*. He rehearseth three manner of joys. First they be joyful whose sins be done away by contrition, which may be called the inward joy for the grant of their petition. Secondly they be more glad when their sins be covered and put out of knowledge by confession; and this may be called the joy shewed outwardly by joyful moving of the body. And thirdly they be most glad when their sins be so clean done away by satisfaction, that no token may be seen or known of them; and this may be called the joy ever to be exercised in the laud and praise of God for His merciful goodness. The prophet applieth the two first joys to rightwise people. They may be called rightwise which have very contrition with a full purpose to be confessed; or else they be called rightwise that after very contrition had, and whole confession made, be assoiled clean from sin of[1] their ghostly father; for they be justified by the sacrament of penance which took efficacy and strength by the Blood and Passion of Christ. They be called *Recti corde* that have made satisfaction so plentifully that God can ask no more of them. For this our prophet saith *Lætamini in Domino et exultate justi: et gloriamini omnes recti corde:* " Ye that be made rightwise by very contrition and true confession, joy in our Lord. And ye that be made perfect by due satisfaction, joy ye eternally in our Lord."

THE THIRD PENITENTIAL PSALM.
DOMINE NE IN FURORE.

PSALM xxxvii (Part I)

MARVEL nothing although we begin not our sermon with the Third Penitential Psalm in order. For or ever we took upon us to declare the two first Penitential Psalms, our promise was somewhat to speak of the Nativity of our Blessed Lady at the day; which purpose willing to keep (also desired of our friends to follow the order of the Psalms, though it seemed to be hard for us so to do), notwithstanding, by the help of our Blessed Lady we have attempted the matter, and made the first part of this Psalm to agree with our first purpose.

QUÆ EST ISTA QUÆ PROGREDITUR QUASI AURORA CONSURGENS?[2]

AFTER the offence of our first fathers, Adam and Eve, all the world was confounded many years by darkness and the night of sin; of the which darkness and night a remembrance is made in holy Scripture oftentimes.

[1] by.   [2] Cant. 6.

Notwithstanding, many that were the very servants and worshippers of Almighty God, to whom the said darkness and night of sin was very irksome and grievous, had admonition that the very Sun of Rightwiseness should spring upon all the world and shine to their great and singular comfort and make a marvellous clear day. As the prophet Zachary said and prophesied of Christ *Visitavit nos oriens ex alto, illuminare his qui in tenebris et in umbra mortis sedent:* "Our Blessed Lord hath visited us from above to give light unto them which sit in darkness and in the shadow of death." Also Christ in the Gospel of John saith *Abraham vidit diem meum et gavisus est:* "Abraham saw My day, whereby he was made glad and joyful." The natural day which we behold should rather of congruence be called the day of the sun, of whom he hath his beginning, than our day. So this spiritual day wherein spiritually we live under the Christian faith, which by the Sun of Rightwiseness hath brought forth Jesus Christ, should be called more properly the day of Him than of us. Christ our Saviour called it His day saying *Vidit diem meum:* "Abraham saw My day." Abraham saw not the present day of Christ as the Apostles did; he had only the sight of it in his soul by true hope that it should come. Notwithstanding, he and many others desired greatly to see this spiritual Sun and the clear day of it. Our Saviour said to His Apostles *Multi reges et prophetæ voluerunt videre quæ vos videtis; et non viderunt:* "Many kings and prophets would fain have seen the mystery of Mine Incarnation which ye see, and yet they did not." And what marvel was it if they that lay in darkness and in the blind night of sin wherein no pleasure was to sleep, did take no rest[1] to desire fervently and abide the springing of the bright Sun, our Saviour? Holy Fathers before the Incarnation, which marvellously irked and despised the works of darkness and the night of sin, every one of them daily and continually prayed that the very Sun of Rightwiseness might spring in their time. Nevertheless their good hope and trust of it was deferred many years; and

[1] never cease.

at the last when time was behovable and convenient in the
sight of Almighty God. He caused this clear Sun for to
give light unto the world. Notwithstanding, it was done
in a just and due order. For of a truth it had not been
seeming and well ordered that after so great and horrible
darkness of the night, the marvellous clearness of this
Sun should have been shewed immediately. It was according of very right that first a morning should come
between, which was not so dark as the night, neither so
clear as the Sun. This order agreeth both to Nature,
Scripture and reason. First, by the order of nature we
perceive that between the darkness of the night and the
clear light of the day, a certain mean[1] light cometh between; the which we call the morning. It is more lighter
and clearer than is the night, albeit the sun is much more
clearer than it. Every man knoweth this thing well, for
daily we have it in experience. Holy Scripture also
teacheth that in the beginning of the world when heaven
and earth should be created, all things were covered with
darkness a long season; and or ever the sun in his very
clearness gave light to the world, a certain mean light
was made which had place between darkness and the very
clear light of the sun. This is well shewed by Moses
in the beginning of Genesis. Reason also, which
searcheth the knowledge of many causes, findeth when one
thing is changed into his contrary, as from cold to heat,
it is done first by certain means or by certain alterations
coming between. Water, which of its nature is very cold,
is not suddenly by the fire made hot to the uttermost; but
first cometh between a little warmness, as we might say
lukewarm, which is neither very hot nor very cold, but in
a mean between both. An apple also which first is green
waxeth not suddenly yellow; but first it is somewhat
white, between green and yellow indifferent. Thus we
perceive by reason that it was not convenient this great
clearness of the Sun our Saviour should have been shewed
so soon and immediately after the so fearful and dark
night of sin, without rising of the morning, which is a
mean between both. Since it is so then that just and

[1] intermediate.

right order will it be so, and also it is according for a wise man so to order it, who will doubt but that the wisdom of our Lord God, unable to be shewed,[1] kept this due and reasonable order namely in His work, whereby *salutem operatus est in medio terræ:* " He wrought health in the midst of the earth?" Sith also He kept the same in all His operations, as St. Paul witnesseth, saying *Quæcunque ordinata sunt, a Deo sunt:* " All things well ordered be by the ordinance of Almighty God." Furthermore, because this matter should be expressed more openly, we shall endeavour ourselves to shew by the three reasons afore rehearsed, that this blessed Lady, Mother to our Saviour, may well be called a morning, since before her none was without sin. After her the most clear Sun, Christ Jesus, shewed His light to the world, expulsing utterly by His innumerable clearness these darknesses wherein all the world was wrapped and covered before. We see by experience the morning riseth out of darkness, as the Wise Man saith: *Deus qui dixit lucem de tenebris splendescere:* " Almighty God commandeth light to shine out of darkness." The clerk Orpheus marvelled greatly of it saying *O nox quæ lucem emittis:* " O dark night, I marvel sore that thou bringeth forth light." And of a truth it is marvel to man's reason that light should spring out of darkness. So in like manner we may marvel of this Blessed Virgin, she being clean without spot of any manner sin, notwithstanding should spring and originally come of sinners that were covered and wrapped in darkness and the night of sin. Also, after the morning the sun ariseth, in manner as it were brought forth and had his beginning of the morning: likewise our Saviour Christ Jesus was born and brought forth of this Blessed Virgin and spread His light over all the world. We also perceive, like as the sun riseth of the morning and maketh it more clear by the effusion of his light, so Christ Jesus born of this Virgin defiled her not with any manner spot of sin, but endued and repleted her with much more light and grace than she had before. Last, although it seemeth the morning to be cause of the sun, notwithstanding, the

---

[1] inexpressible.

sun without doubt is cause of it. And in like wise, although this blessed Virgin brought forth our Saviour
Jesus, yet He made her and was cause of her bringing
into this world. Thus ye perceive by nature that this
blessed Virgin may well be likened to a morning. The
same shall be shewed if we rehearse the order of Scripture. It is spoken in Genesis that first Almighty God
made heaven and earth. The earth was void and deso-
late, all was covered with darkness, and the spirit of
God was borne aloft. Then Almighty God commanded,
the first day, by His word only, that light should be
made; and anon light was made, and after that the fourth
day the sun was created. This we read in the beginning
of Genesis. But let us now shew what it signifieth for
our purpose. First heaven and earth may signify to us
man and woman, for the woman is subject to the man,
like as the earth is to heaven. Woman is also barren and
lacking fruit without the help of man, and the earth without the influence of heaven is barren and void of all fruit.
Semblably,[1] every generation of man from the creation of
Adam was wrapped and covered with the darkness of
sin; and though the spirit of God was ever aloft ready
to give grace, for all that, none was found able to receive
it unto the time this blessed Virgin was ordained by the
Holy Trinity to spring and to be brought forth into the
world. Which by the providence of Almighty God was
surely kept and defended from every spot and blemish
of sin, so that we may well say unto her: *Tota pulchra es,
amica mea, et macula non est in te:* "O Blessed Lady,
thou art all fair and without spot or blemish of sin."
The angel at her salutation said: *Ave plena gratia:* "Hail
full of grace." This blessed Virgin, full of the beams
of grace, was ordained by God as a light of the morning,
and afterwards brought forth the bright shining Sun with
His manifold beams, our Saviour Christ: *Qui illuminat
omnem hominem venientem in hunc mundum:* "Which
giveth light to every creature coming to this world."
Take heed how conveniently it agreeth with holy Scripture, this Virgin to be called a morning. Also whereas

[1] similarly.

reason, of a congruence, will that between two contraries a mean must be had, maketh marvellously well that this Virgin may be called a morning; for like as the morning is a mean between the great clearness of the sun and the ugsome[1] darkness of the night, so this blessed and holy Virgin is the mean between this bright Sun our Saviour and wicked sinners, and a partaker of both, for she is the Mother of God's Son and also the Mother of sinners. For when our Saviour Christ hanged upon the cross, He commended and left to this blessed Virgin St. John the Evangelist as her son, saying to her: *Mulier, ecce filius tuus:* "Woman behold thy son." And unto St. John He said: *Ecce mater tua:* "Behold thy Mother." John by interpretation is to say 'the grace of God,' signifying that by God's grace, and not by their own merits, sinners be made the inheritors of the Heavenly Kingdom. Sinners therefore be commended to this Virgin Mary as to a Mother; she is Mother of sinners. St. Austin saith: " It seemeth to be a noble kindred between this blessed Virgin and sinners, for she received all her goodness for sinners; sin was cause why she was made the Mother of God." Also if we have taken any goodness, we have it all by her. Therefore of very right this holy Virgin Mary is the Mother of sinners. All Christ's Church calleth her *Mater miserorum:* "the Mother of wretched sinners." She is also the Mother of mercy, for Christ is very mercy. The prophet, speaking of Him, saith thus *Deus meus misericordia mea:* " My God and my mercy." Christ is very mercy; she is the Mother of Christ, therefore the Mother of mercy: for this cause, as we said before, she must needs be a mean between the mercy of God and the wretchedness of sin; between Christ most innocent and wretched sinners; between the shining light and black darkness. She is also the mean between the bright sun of the day and the dark cloud of the night. None was born before her without sin, either mortal, venial or original. Many before were men of great virtue and holiness, as Jeremy and Elias with other, but because they were not clean without every spot of sin, their vir-

[1] ugly.

tue and holiness was hid in manner as under a cloud.
And the holy angels remembering this matter, beholding
this light to shew forth without any spot of darkness
after so long continuance of the dark night of sin, said
each one to other with an admiration or marvelling *Quæ
est ista quæ progreditur quasi aurora consurgens?* "What
is she which goeth forth as a rising morning?" Therefore since this blessed Lady Mary as a morning goeth
between our night and the day of Christ, between our
darkness and His brightness, and last, between the misery
of our sins and the mercy of God, what other help should
rather be to wretched sinners whereby they might sooner
be delivered from their wretchedness and come to mercy,
than by the help of this blessed Virgin Mary?   Who
may come or attain from one extremity unto another without a mean between both?   Let us therefore acknowledge
to her our wretchedness, ask her help: she cannot but
hear us, for she is our Mother; she shall speak for us
unto her merciful Son and ask His mercy, and without
doubt He shall grant her petition, which is His Mother
and the Mother of mercy.   Let us therefore call unto
her saying: " O most holy Virgin, thou art the Mother
of God, Mother of mercy, the Mother also of wretched
sinners and their singular help, comfort to all sorrowful; vouchsafe to hear our wretchedness and provide a
convenient and behovable remedy for the same." But
what miseries shall we most specially shew unto her?
Truly the common wretchedness of all sinners, which the
Church hath taught us often to have in remembrance,
which also the prophet David hath described in the third
Penitential Psalm whereof we shall now speak.   And as
the woman of Canaan when she prayed to our Lord was
not heard anon; notwithstanding, His disciples having
pity and compassion, spake to Christ their Master for
her: so we now, lest peradventure our merciful Lord
heard not our prayers in the other Psalms before because
of our grievous sins, let us turn our prayer to his most
merciful Mother, beseeching her to shew mercy and call
to Almighty God for us as our advocate.

QUÆ EST ISTA QUÆ PROGREDITUR QUASI AURORA CONSURGENS?

WE shall mark three conditions of the morning which may well be applied to this blessed Virgin. First, if the morning be fair, it is mild and quiet without trouble of wind, storms or tempest. Also by little and little it riseth upward above the darkness, putting away the black cloud of the night. Thirdly it is bright and clear without clouds or mists. This bright and holy Virgin had all these conditions. First, she was meek and mild in her soul, so that neither blast of pride, neither storm of wrath was in her, but always she was gentle, lowly and meek. Secondly, she enhanced herself far above the darkness of sin, putting under foot the occasion of it; she also broke his head, which was the cause and increaser of sin. Thirdly, she was a bright and clear Virgin without all darkness of ignorance. Of these conditions many things may be said to the laud and praise of this blessed Virgin, if we intended so to do. But our purpose is otherwise set: our mind at this time is not to speak of her lauds which no creature can sufficiently express, but we purpose to make our prayers to that blessed Mother and Maid, that she of her goodness vouchsafe to help us in our miseries. For in us be three kinds of wretchedness, contrary to the three virtues in her spoken of before. First, the misery of fear and dread, whereby our soul is never in rest but always troubled and shaken with that great storm and tempest. Secondly, the misery of bondage and servitude to sin, that is when any person is made subject and cast down by the great weight of it. Thirdly, the misery of ignorance and blindness, whereby the light of truth and good knowledge is withdrawn from us and hid as under a cloud. Let us now therefore ask help of this most holy Virgin which obtaineth qualities and conditions alway contrary to these miseries. All these wretchednesses be rehearsed of the prophet David in this third Penitential Psalm, as ye shall understand by diligent giving heed to our sayings. Many troubles and vexations arise in us against the tranquillity of this mild morning; some cometh by fear of the eternal punishments of God, some for dread of the pains of Purgatory, some be caused of our bodily diseases which we suffer for the guilt and offence of our first father Adam, some by the remembrance of death uncertain that needs must follow at the last after all these grievous vexations. Many also be caused by fear of the temporal punishment of God exercised in this life for our trespasses; and last by the ugsomeness of our sins many tribulations be engendered in our souls, by the which sins we have deserved punishment of God's vengeance. Of a truth one of these vexations some time troubleth the minds of sinners. Our prophet remembereth them by order.

The first perturbation or trouble which is caused by fear of the punishment of God everlastingly to be used upon damned sinners, must needs prick the mind and conscience of the sinner; for when that eternal punishment shall appear and be shewed, the countenance of God shall be so formidable and fearful that in the time when miserable sinners shall stand in His sight they shall think themself set in a burning furnace of fire. As it is said in holy Scripture: *Pones eos ut clibanum ignis in tempore vultus tui:* "Blessed Lord, Thou shalt at the day of Judgment set all wretched sinners as a clew (or a great heap) of fire for fear of beholding Thy fearful countenance." The word which He shall speak to them at that time shall be so sharp and vehemently biting, in so much they shall covet or desire rather to die a thousand times than to hear it, when He shall openly give sentence upon them saying *Discedite a me, maledicti, in ignem æternum qui paratus est diabolo et angelis eius:* "Go from Me, ye cursed sinners, into everlasting fire, which is prepared for the devil and his angels." O marvellous sharp saying! O word more piercing than a double-edged sword! What creature shall not fear to be separated from the face of God, from heavenly glory, from the fellowship and company of saints, and to be cast down into eternal fire with those fearful and cruel devils? The prophet therefore fearing this everlasting punishment, beginneth his Psalm crying to Almighty God, saying *Domine ne in furore tuo arguas me:* "Blessed Lord, punish me not in Thine everlasting punishment." Let us do in like manner, making our prayers to this blessed Virgin, saying: "O blessed Lady, be thou mean and mediatrice between thy Son and wretched sinners, that He punish us not everlastingly."

If peradventure we be delivered by the infinite mercy of God from crucifying in the fire of Hell, yet there is another fire to be feared, that is to say the fire of Purgatory, which fire is so hot and full of diversity of pain, that all torments and diseases of this world be nothing compared to it; which thing holy St. Austin confirmeth by these words, saying *Ille ignis gravior est quam quicquid homo pati potest in hac vita:* "The fire of Purgatory is more grievous than any pain man may suffer in this life." Alas we wretched sinners, what hard saying is this? Be there not some grievous pains in this life? Those that be vexed with the stone, strangury, and the flux, feel they not marvellous great pains when they cannot keep themself from wailing and crying out for sorrow? What shall I say of them which suffer pain in the head, toothache, and aching of bones? Do they not suffer great pains? And also martyrs, of whom many were slain, some boiled, another sawed in two, another torn with wild beasts, another roasted on the fire, another put into scalding hot pitch and rosin, did they not suffer bitter pain? Notwithstanding, to be punished in the fire of Purgatory is far more grievous pain than all these we have rehearsed. What marvel is it then if the fear of so great and painful fire trouble us sinners? Wherefore it followeth: *Et ne in ira tua corripias me:* "Blessed Lord," said David, "correct me not in the fire of Purgatory." So let us call unto our blessed Lady, praying her to be mean[1] for us that her Son, our Judge, not only punish us not in the pains of Hell which be everlasting, but also that He correct us not in the pains of Purgatory which have an end.

The third trouble that we suffer riseth and is caused of the wounds inflicted and being in our body for the sin

[1] mediatrix.

of our first parents. For when Adam was set in Paradise, a place of great pleasure, volupty and rest, Almighty God threatened him saying, whatsoever time he tasted of the forbidden tree, he should be wounded: *Quod tam ei quam universæ posteritati eius mortem injerret:* " Which should be a mortal wound both to him and all his posterity." Almighty God had His bow ready bent wherewith He should strike him; of the which bow is written in another place *Tetendit arcum suum:* " God hath bent His bow." For all this, Adam, attempted the matter, fell to sin; whom anon Almighty God did smite. The vehemence of the which stroke, all we that came of him do feel; the wounds of it abide still in us, not clean made whole, although they be hid and covered. Will ye know which be the wounds? Let us be hungry a little while, and anon we shall feel the penury of hunger. Abstain from drink: anon cometh thirst. Go afoot many miles: anon cometh weariness. Put your finger nigh the fire, and full soon shall ye feel impassible[1] heat. Eat unwholesome meats, and anon cometh sickness. By these wounds aforesaid without doubt we be brought to death, if the body be not soon remedied. Adam wanted[2] all these wounds or ever Almighty God did strike him. And we also should have wanted them if that stroke had not been. We all be wounded by his stroke, wherefore the prophet saith *Quoniam sagittæ tuæ infixæ sunt mihi:* " Blessed Lord, Thine arrows be sticked in me."

If peradventure these arrows might be plucked away by any medicine, or by craft, we might be made whole of our wounds, and so to escape death, whose fear troubleth us without measure in this fourth place. The Wise Man saith *O mors, quam amara homini habenti pacem in substantia sua:* " O death, how bitter art thou to a man having peace with his substance of worldly goods "; or else thus, " that hath this world at his will." Which[3] use these worldly pleasures merrily, they know not, they have not in mind what is behind in the world to come. Alas how grievous and bitter is to them the remembrance of death, whose darts or arrows may not be expulsed by any

---

[1] unendurable.   [2] was free from.   [3] They who.

craft! We cannot find the means by any medicine to heal our wounds, we must needs die, and daily we draw nigh death more and more. *Omnes morimur:* "All we die, or be dying," Scripture saith. This verb *morior*, after[1] St. Augustine, is undeclined, signifying that no creature may escape, flee or decline from death: our Lord hath so grievously stricken us with the dint of His arrows. Wherefore our prophet saith *Et confirmasti super me manum tuam:* "Lord, Thou hast pierced and fixed Thine arrows so sore in me that my wound is so great and without cure, I cannot escape, but must needs die."

We said the fifth perturbation cometh for fear of God's punishment, which the prophet calleth in this Psalm *faciem iræ Dei.* For by these words *furorem Dei* is understood the everlasting punishment upon them which be damned. By these words *faciem iræ Dei* is understood temporal punishment in this life; which temporal punishments causeth us also to be in trouble. For what creature, remembering so many punishments done upon sinners in this life bodily, and peradventure for less offences than he himself hath done, can be without fear, lest he should suffer the same or more grievous for his own offences? Adam against the commandment of God tasted but one apple, and anon he was cast out from the goodly garden of Paradise into this earth full of briars and brambles. It seemeth but a small matter, and also[2] he, and all his posterity ever after, were made mortal. Alas, how many times have we sinners broken the commandments of God. The people of Israel, led by Moses through the desert, when it was so they had eaten no flesh of many days, at the last they desired to eat of the Egyptians' flesh, like as it was their customable meat before. Almighty God gave them their desire. But *quoniam adhuc esca fuit in ore eorum ira Dei descendit super eos:* "Whilst they were eating and meat in their mouth, the punishment of God fell upon them," and a great part of them were slain. Afterwards the same people, made weary by a long journey, grudged in their minds against our Lord; wherefore sudden fire fell upon

---

[1] according to.   [2] yet.

E

them, and utterly burnt and destroyed the latter part of
their host. Have we not committed many more grievous
offences than these be? Yes truly. For when we lacked
no meat but had great plenty of it, have we not for all
that desired more delicate meats, not content with such
as we had? Hath not a little bodily labour been tedious
to us, as to go unto the church, there to abide to be at
the service of God, and to hear wholesome doctrine?
Which of us hearing these offences, being culpable in
them, will not fear the punishments of God both in this
life and after? Namely when this holy prophet so did,
insomuch he saith his flesh trembleth for fear. *Non est
sanitas in carne mea:* " Blessed Lord, I have none health
in my flesh, it trembleth for fear of Thy punishments."
They be very happy and blessed which never defiled
themself with sin, but always hath kept them clean
without any spot of it, as touching actual sin, for truly
they have great rest in their souls; and they that have
done the contrary, feel in themselves an inward strife,
when they remember themself in their living: for such
as hath a polluted conscience give them to other business
than to look upon themself. Truly the abomination
of an unclean conscience is so great that the remembrance
of it is thought to that person so encumbered so great
pain, as he were vexed and troubled in the torments of
Hell. O how many hath slain themself after their great
offences done, when they might not hold up and sustain
their unhappy life! Example we have of a Roman
woman called Lucrece and many other. The three prin-
cipal parts of the soul whereby the whole man should
be governed, beholding the ugsome and detestable monster of sin, doth accuse each one the other. To
the Memory it is objected that he should have kept in
mind the holy admonitions and teachings which oftentimes be heard by the preachers of godly doctrine; to
the Reason is said that he should have resisted and withstood more busily, and not have suffered so great filthiness of sin to be committed in the soul; to the Will is
objected that by his boldness and running too much upon
his own bridle, neither obeying to Memory nor to Reason,

is caused that the soul is polluted with the filthiness of sin. Therefore the conscience always pricketh and grudgeth against sins evil committed, according to the prophet's saying: *Non est pax ossibus meis a facie peccatorum:* " No part of my body can be in rest for the grievousness of my sins." Take heed with how many and what storms of tribulation we be vexed within our bodies: we have no tranquillity, no quietness, but troubled in every part with many divers vexations. First by the pains of Hell, of Purgatory, by our bodily grievance, by death, by the punishment of God, and last by the abomination of our sin.

Therefore let us go unto this mild morning, our blessed Lady Virgin Mary, beseeching her that she will vouchsafe to deliver us from these stormy wretchednesses in this life, and after grant us quiet souls.

These sufficeth for the first kind of wretchedness. We said the second kind of misery is to be cast down under the darkness and cloud of sin, and miserably to be in captivity under the yoke of it. Many times sin is compared to a serpent. A serpent hath a head, a body and a tail; semblably so hath sin, for when any man feeleth the first instigation or stirring to sin, doubtless there is the serpent's head. When afterwards he consenteth to the same instigation, then he suffereth the body of that serpent to enter. And at last when he fulfilleth the sin in deed, then is the venomous tail of the serpent entered. Without thou resist and withstand the head, that is to say the first suggestion, it shall be very hard for thee to exclude sin; for whereas a serpent may get in his head, anon he bringeth after the residue of his body. So by sin, if also the straight passage be made open to the first admonition or stirring of sin, anon he draweth after him the whole body, and never ceaseth till it come into the highest part of the soul. He advanceth himself and is lifted up far above the mind, which ought to be the head of the soul. And this of a truth is a great misery, whereof this holy prophet David maketh his complaint saying *Quoniam iniquitates meæ supergressæ sunt caput meum:* " All the parts of my body be without rest because my sins be exalted far above mine head." We have given so great licence to this serpent sin, and so easily entreated[1] it, that now when it is once entered it will not out again, but, as a tyrant, hath decreed to keep in possession the habitacle that he hath won, either peaceably or by strength. First or ever we committed sin, many motions of it were felt in us, but it was only in the inferior part of the soul. And now since it is suffered to have any interest, he hath enhanced himself above the highest part of the soul and there is resident, commanding what him list,[2] thrusting down the poor soul with his grievous burden and weight, that oftentimes it is compelled to do that thing which it would not do. Peradventure some sinner will say, " I perceive nor feel any weight in myself, do I never so many sins." To whom we answer that if a dog, having a great stone bound about his neck, be cast down from a high tower, he feeleth no weight of that stone as long as he is falling down, but when he is once fallen to the ground he is burst all to pieces by reason of that weight. So the sinner going down towards the pit of Hell feeleth not the great burden of sin, but when he shall come into the depths of Hell he shall feel more pain than he would. Also every creature which is about to put away the yoke of sin feeleth the great and grievous weight of it. Our holy prophet had in experience the heavy burden of sin, who said *Et sicut onus grave gravatæ sunt super me:* " My sins be heavy upon me like to a heavy burden." God forbid that we say no man may cast out sin from the soul once entered into it. We say not that, for if it were so, all we should despair. Because why? No person is without sin. But we say it is right hard utterly to expulse sin, suffered so long at liberty, and hath had so much licence to abide in the soul; and holy doctors acknowledge the same. And St. Anselm, whose words cometh now first to mind, saith *O peccata, quam felices aditus habetis et quam difficiles exitus:* " O ye foul sins, how glad and easy enterings have ye into man's soul, and how hard be your goings out from it." Sins may be

[1] dealt with.   [2] he pleases.

expulsed, but how? Truly by great contrition, diligent confession, and not a little bodily satisfaction. But after that our sins be so done away, if we take not upon us mightily to withstand and make battle against them, likely they shall enter again into the soul. And, as our Saviour saith, *Erunt novissima hominis illius deteriora prioribus:* "Then shall we be in worse conditions far than we were before." Then shall the wounds of our sins wax raw again; then shall the tokens[1] where they were fixed wax rotten afresh by our foolishness and negligence. Of the which misery David complaineth in this place, saying *Putruerunt et corruptæ sunt cicatrices meæ a facie insipientiæ meæ:* "The old tokens of my sins wax rotten again by mine own foolishness." He that is inured and encumbered with these evils, shall we not call him wretched and unhappy? Yes, truly, for nothing else but sin may make a man wretched. Be a man never so poor and needy, if he be without sin, yet he is blessed and happy. Solomon saith *Miseros facit populos peccatum:* "Sin maketh wretched people." St. Paul, having the same misery in experience, said *Infelix ego homo, quis me liberabit de corpore mortis huius?* " I, unhappy man, who shall deliver me from the danger of this deadly misery of sin?" Socrates was asked a question (as it appeareth in the Gorgias of Plato) of one named Polus, whether Archelaus, which then had in governance the kingdom of Macedonia in great glory, were happy and blessed or not. Socrates answered him he could not tell: " It is to me uncertain." Then said Polus, " He is a king." Socrates said, " Although he so be, yet may he be a wretch." Polus added more and said, " He hath a glorious kingdom, a great household, and great riches." Socrates answered, " What of all this? These commodities maketh not a man blessed, for under them may be privily a wretched soul. If thou wilt," said Socrates, " that I tell thee whether this man be blessed or wretched, show me his soul, and anon I shall assoil[2] thy question, for the demonstration of this matter dependeth of the soul." Truly a soul subject to sin is wretched, which our

[1] scars.   [2] solve.

prophet David witnesseth, saying, *Miser factus sum:* " By the reason of my sin I am made a wretch." That creature, whatsoever he be, is blessed whose will is obedient to reason, that is to say, in whom reason and grace hath domination; for by reason and grace right and justice shall be kept. But if it be contrary, then shall perversity and unrightwiseness have place and liberty. That we may more openly perceive this thing, let us consider this example. As long as the middle of a line is equal with both ends, neither going wrong towards the right hand nor towards the left hand, so long it is called a right line; but if it turn contrary either to the one part or to the other, or lift up itself above either ends, the line is not right but crooked. In like manner let us consider the powers in the soul, that is to say reason, will, and understanding. The understanding must be guided by the will, and the will must be ruled by reason; for the will is the middle part between understanding and reason, like as the middle point in a line. Wherefore if the will, which ought to be the middle part, and also subdued to reason, lift up itself above reason, is not the order perverse and inconvenient? Is not there a crooked soul? Yes, without doubt. Likewise it is in sinners when reason is put down and will is unwisely, exalted. *Et incurvatus sum usque in finem.* The prophet saith: " By sin I am made crooked unto the ground. I have more mind on earthly things than upon heavenly." When the soul is thus deformed and brought into this miserable condition, what is left behind but penance and sorrow? The philosophers shewed two divers ways: one is the way of virtue, the other of vice. The way that leadeth a man to virtue is laborious and full of thorns; notwithstanding, the end of it is very pleasant. The way which bringeth a man to vice is merry and full of sensual pleasures, but the end of it is very bitter and sharp. A certain philosopher called Demosthenes what time he desired to have the preference and company of a certain evil-disposed woman, and she asked a great sum of money; he answered that his learning was not to buy penance so dear. Signifying that after the filthy volupty of the flesh nothing remaineth but sorrow and penance, for the which he would not give so much money. Our prophet considering this addeth, saying *Tota die contristatus ingrediebar*. Many causes there be for sinners to be penitent which have cast down themself into these miseries, not compelled by violence, but by their own will and mind, from the which they may scantly and with great difficulty arise, what for the tyranny of sin, what for leaving of the occasions to sin, caused of the pleasure which the flesh hath gotten by wicked custom of it. For, as St. Jerome saith, those that be virgins feel not so great temptations of the flesh as they which once or ofttimes have had the fleshly volupty in experience; for the flesh that before hath been polluted by the foul and filthy pleasure of the body, feeleth much more unclean motions than doth the flesh which alway hath been clean and chaste; for the unclean body persuadeth and sheweth to the soul the wicked cogitations and dark phantasies of his unthrifty fleshly pleasures done before: whereby it is many times beguiled and scorned. Therefore the prophet saith *Quoniam lumbi mei impleti sunt illusionibus:* "The parts of my flesh wherein the nourishing of fleshly volupty be resident and abiding, are replete and fulfilled with mocks and scorns." O foolish and mad flesh which enticeth and causeth so many evils to the hurt of itself! For the body stirreth and moveth the soul oftentimes to the filthy lust of the flesh, which is the most hurt that can be to the body: for the lively spirits whereby the flesh is quickened be spilt and shed out with the seed of man. And so by that he loseth many of his strengths. Physicians say that a man taketh more hurt by the effusion of a little seed than by shedding of ten times so much blood, which things of a likelihood St. Paul meant rebuking fornicators, saying *Peccatum quodcumque fecerit homo extra corpus suum est; qui autem fornicatur, in corpus suum peccat;* "Every sin that a man doth is outward from his body, but he that doth fornication or lechery offendeth God and also hurteth his body." Verily it is a great misery to love the body so much, and notwithstanding procure so great hurt to it by fleshly lust. Which misery our prophet sheweth, saying *Et non est sanitas in carne mea:* " By the reason of fleshly lust I have no health in my body or in my·flesh." Therefore sin grieveth both body and soul and profiteth none of them, but engendereth great hurt to both. The soul is tormented by a sight of a polluted conscience, by the victory of sin having domination, by the heavy burden of it, by renewing of old sins, by the misery that followeth, by the crooked custom of it once left and forsaken, and last by penance sorrowful. The body is also tormented by the pricking of fleshly lust, and by loss of his strength. So that a sinner may safely say as the prophet writeth following *Afflictus sum:* " I am troubled by sin both in body and soul." The increase of a sinner's pain is when he calleth to remembrance how long he hath served so uncourteous and ungentle a lord. St. John saith *Qui facit enim peccatum, servus est peccati:* " He that committeth sin is the servant of sin." Therefore every sinner hath sin for his lord whom he serveth. What manner of lord sin is may be known by the stipend and reward that he giveth to his servants in the end. St. Paul writeth of this stipend, saying *Stipendia peccati mors est:* " The reward of sin is death." What manner death? Truly death eternal. This reward agreeth well for such a lord. What stipend should the most unhappy lord give but the worst that may be thought? Whosoever serveth this malicious and cursed lord is in great bondage and servitude: wherefore the prophet addeth, saying *Et humiliatus sum nimis:* " By sin I am made a bond man." To whom? Verily to the lord named Sin. Now ye have heard how many great miseries we suffer under the bondage and yoke of sin, and how we be thrust down under the cloud and darkness of sin. Therefore let us flee unto our bright morning, the most holy Mother of God, which as a fair morning hath lifted up herself above all darkness, and by her humility hath broken the devil's head, which was the first author and causer of sin and darkness. Let us ask and trust help of her in this second kind of wretchedness, whereof we have now spoken, alway following the words and order of the prophet.

The third kind of misery is yet behind, which we said is the misery of ignorance and blindness, whereby the light of truth is turned away from us, as by a cloud coming between. This blindness may be shewed many ways, as first by the two means whereof we shall speak: that is to say, we abstain not from sin, neither for the abominable loathsomeness of it, nor for the reverence of our blessed Lord God, alway being present. That thing must needs of very right be thought ugsome and detestable, which is the cause of so many great miseries and bitternesses afore rehearsed; for neither the pains of Hell nor of Purgatory had never been thought, if sin had not been. Mankind should never have felt any weariness or bodily grievance by the reason of labour, if sin had not been; neither any distemperance of cold or heat that should annoy the body, hunger, thirst, no grief of sickness or of violent stroke, if sin had not been. Also the soul should have wanted[1] ignorance, inconstancy, and rebellion of understanding against reason. These miseries and many more which now I leave of[2] happen to us because of sin. Nothing in the world displeaseth Almighty God but sin. For as Moses saith *Vidit Deus cuncta quæ fecerat: et erant valde bona:* "Almighty God looked and saw all things which He made, and they were very good." Every creature of God is good and acceptable to Him if sin be away. But if it be never so goodly a creature defiled with sin, it is abominable in the sight of God, and far more abominable than is the stinking carrion of a dog or any other venomous worm in the sight of men. Wherefore holy Scripture commandeth every person, saying *Quasi a facie colubri fuge peccatum:* "Flee sin like as thou would flee from the sight of an adder or any other venomous worm." And the holy man St. Anselm saith: *Si ex una parte Gehenna fuerit et ex altera peccatum, mallem in Gehennam ire quam inquinari peccato:* "If Hell were of the one side of me and sin on the other side, I had liefer go into Hell than to be defiled with sin": the abominable stink of it is so great. Therefore our blindness is very miserable, which so many times

[1] been without.   [2] say no more about.

have heard of[1] the preachers of God how deadly and horrible a monster sin is, and how much it is to be fled and despised; notwithstanding, we do not eschew it, but studiously with all our diligence follow, clip[2] and in manner kiss it. And when we have none occasion to sin we sorrow and wail. There was never hungry lion that lay so sore a-wait for his prey, as sinners doth to get occasions to sin; they seek the flatterings of worldly pleasures even as ramping lions doth for their prey. Also if they be deferred from their purpose they wail and make sorrow: which misery our prophet shewed in this next verse: *Rugiebam a gemitu cordis mei:* " I sought occasion to sin, not feignedly but from the very heart of me."

This is a great blindness that we have spoken of, and the other which we shall shew is much more. If the loathsomeness of sin be not sufficient to cause us leave and flee from it, at the least the presence of Almighty God, our Maker, our Governor, should cause us forsake sin: in Whose power resteth our life and death, Which from above looketh and beholdeth whatsoever we do, so openly as I see and behold any of you, and much more openly, for if man's aspects or sight might come from the soul and pierce through a glass, through the heavens unto the stars, till it come to the place where Almighty God is resident, notwithstanding, much more the sight of God hath power to look through them all down till it come to the furtherest and inward parts of the heart and soul. I beseech you let us think in ourself: the clearer sight the further may look and behold; and yet, if another be twice so clear, it may perceive and behold twice so far, and so infinitely. Therefore Almighty God, whose sight is far brighter and more clear than all other be, may behold and look to every distance, be it never so far and without number. A great difference is between the sight of God and of man. The farther that man's sight goeth, the more weak and feeble it is. Why? For it is limited at a certain.[3] The sight of God is of great strength without end and limiting at cer-

[1] from. [2] hug. [3] a certain point.

tainty; and for that cause whithersoever it goeth forth, be the space or distance never so far, it is always of like strength and power in every place without change or making less: which holy Scripture witnesseth, saying *Attingit a fine usque ad finem fortiter:* "The sight of God attaineth to every distance from end to end strongly, or always alike strong." And in another place of Scripture it is said *Nulla creatura est invisibilis in conspectu illius, omnia autem nuda et aperta sunt oculis eius:* "No creature is invisible in the sight of God, all things be naked and open to His eyes." Therefore it is a great and miserable blindness when we will not behold and see the horrible and fearful countenance of sin. And truly it is a more great and miserable blindness not to fear the sight of the Most High Lord God Almighty, but, He looking upon us from Whom nothing may be hid, to have the desire of so loathsome and foul thing in our heart as sin is, if we remember not and be in will to sorrow and wail for it. O great darkness! O dim cloud! O very thick mist which suffers not the light of truth to shine upon sinners! Let us therefore run to our most bright and clear Morning, Mary the Mother of God, which is without all and the least spot of sin. Beseech her meekly that she put away this black cloud and darkness of sin, to the intent we may have grace to loath and fear the filthiness of it, and to dread the presence of our fearful Judge, Almighty God.

Now sith we have satisfied for our purpose at this time, we should leave this place of the Psalm, but that the verse following containeth a rehearsal or epilogue almost of everything spoken before. The prophet saith *Cor meum turbatum est:* "My heart is sore troubled." Take heed and mark here the first kind of wretchedness, that is to say, the tempestuous tribulations wherewith the heart of sinners is troubled and vexed, first for fear of the eternal punishment of God in Hell, for dread of His punishments in Purgatory, also by fear of death hanging alway on our necks, for dread of God's punishment in this life, and last for the ugsomeness of our sins. For these we may say with the prophet *Cor nostrum contur-*

batum est: "Our hearts be sore troubled." It followeth: *Dereliquit me virtus mea:* "My strength hath forsaken me." Here is noted the second kind of misery whereby we be put down miserably under the thraldom of sin, by which thraldom we be overcome, subdued, our old tokens of sin wax rotten again, we be made unhappy, crooked and sorrowful, we be scourged sore and made low as subjects, so that of right we may say: *Dereliquit nos virtus nostra:* "Our strength hath forsaken us." The prophet added *Lumen oculorum meorum et ipsum non est mecum:* "The sight of mine eyes hath failed me." Here is the third kind of wretchedness expressed, that is to say of our cloudy blindness whereby we be so much blinded that neither for the abomination of sin, which is a foul and fearful monster, nor for the reverence of God, being present, we will refrain, but sin still and that grievously. From which miseries the most blessed Virgin deliver us, whose nativity we hallow this day, by her Son Our Lord Jesus Christ, Whom she as a fair Morning brought forth, the most bright Sun, to give light unto all sinners.

THE THIRD PENITENTIAL PSALM.
DOMINE NE IN FURORE.
PSALM xxxvii (Part II)

ALL we Christian people are bound of very duty to give great and immortal thanks to the holy prophet David, which so diligently hath left in writing his Psalms, most godly to be read of us and our posterity. And his so doing, as meseemeth, was most for three causes. First that by these holy Psalms the minds of sinners might be raised up and excited, as by a sweet melody, to receive and take the study and learning of virtue. Secondly, that if any man or woman hath fallen to great and abominable sins, yet they should not despair, but put their whole and steadfast hope of forgiveness in God. Thirdly, that they might use these holy Psalms as letters of supplication and speedful prayers for remission and forgiveness to be purchased of Almighty God.

Pythagorici,[1] the people of that sect or of that usage, were accustomed every morning when they should rise from their beds to hear the sound of a harp, whereby their spirits might be more quick and ready to receive their studies; thinking nothing more profitable than it unto the free and noble exciting of their minds. For doubtless their sluggish and slothful minds by that melody were made quick and merry. Also sometime wicked spirits were chased away by the musical and sweet stroke of the harp. Which thing done is read of King Saul, that when he was vexed and troubled of the wicked spirit, he had his most and only remedy by the harp of David, at whose sound the malign spirit was driven away. It is also thought that the same wicked spirit had so great power on Saul for his sin. So likewise holy Fathers think all sinners to be under the power of an evil spirit. Let us therefore turn again unto these sweet melodies of our prophet David, which some time he sang with his godly harp, whereby we may chase and put away all sluggishness and sloth put into us by wretched spirits. In the which sweet sounds we shall hear so great plenty and diversity of tunes as ever was heard before; for sometime he speaketh of God, sometime of the devil, sometime of holy angels, sometime of damned spirits; now of Hell pains, and sometime of the pains of Purgatory; other whiles of the rightwiseness of God, sometime of His great mercy; now of dread, anon of hope, sometime of sorrow and weeping, and sometime of gladness and comfort; sometime of the soul; sometime of the cursing of vices and sins, sometime of the praising of virtues; otherwhiles of good and rightwise people, and anon of wicked and unrightwise. By this diversity of melody if sinners cannot be raised up from the sleep of sin and excited unto godly watchings, they are to be thought as very dead.

And as we said in the second place, they that be wretched and sinful creatures may trust to have forgive-

---

[1] i.e. the Pythagoreans.

ness of God by these holy Psalms. For every man knoweth this prophet David was a wretched and grievous sinner; nevertheless afterwards he lived holily, and by the merits of his life was lifted up into heaven. The medicine and remedy that he used for doing away his sins was pure and clear penance, which he laboured so much by oft saying these Psalms that anon he was made perfectly clean. Why therefore should we wretched sinners doubt to be made clean from all sins, be they never so grievous, when we know the life before of this prophet unclean with so great filthiness of sin, and now made so bright and without spot of it, by penance which is the very purger of sin? Trowest thou his sin was not grievous? Truly it was; which also himself witnesseth, saying *Peccavi valde:* "I have sinned grievously." Is not the same medicine and remedy which he used, that is to say penance, present and ready at hand to us all? Yes truly, for it was said to every person *Pœnitentiam agite:* "Do penance." Have not we the same God, and is not He as rich and plentiful in His mercy as ever He was before? Yes, without doubt. St. Paul affirmeth the same, saying *Idem Dominus omnium et dives in omnes qui invocant eum:* "The Lord of all is one without change or mutability, and even alike liberal and plenteous to every creature that calleth to Him." Trowest thou that He be partial in any condition, and that He offereth not His grace to every creature over all?[1] Yes, verily. For St. Peter the Apostle saith *In veritate comperi quia non est personarum acceptor Deus, sed in omni gente qui timet Deum et operatur justitiam, hic acceptus est illi:* " I have spied and perceived for a truth that God is none accepter of persons; but amongst all people, whosoever dreadeth Almighty God and doth rightwiseness, that person is acceptable unto Him." Therefore if we dread Almighty God and do rightwise penance, we may trust verily for to have forgiveness of Him, and without doubt for to be accepted of His mercy. Unto the which this holy prophet David both admonisheth and enticeth us by these holy Psalms. The which matter ought for to

[1] generally.

be for all wretched sinners to their great comfort and
trust of forgiveness.

The third and last (that these holy Psalms be like as
letters of supplication the which we may give unto Almighty God as ready movers and stirrers of His infinite
mercy for us) shall be made open on this wise. If peradventure any person have a matter or business with the
King's Highness, and in his cause greatly desire his goodness and pity, will he not shortly go unto some wise man
in such matters and desire a letter of supplication for
to be made diligently, whereby he may cause the King's
pity in his business to be obtained and had?   Truly his
trust is not only in his own wisdom for to be so bold in
handling his matter, and to purpose it only by his own
words or his own wit. We sinners be in like condition.
For truly we have many matters in the high court of
the most high King, Almighty God, for the which
it should be profitable and necessary the pity of God to
be purchased for us.   And who is more wise in that
court for our business to be sped, that is to say for forgiveness to be obtained, than is our prophet David that
committed[1] before the peril and danger of the same thing
in himself?   Verily he was a sinner as we be, and a busy
follower[2] for forgiveness. With great diligence he made
these holy Psalms, which he daily offered up to Almighty
God with great devotion as letters of supplication, by the
which he moved greatly His goodness for to forgive him.
Therefore, we knowing the virtue and efficacy of these
holy Psalms, let us use them in our like business and
doubt not to have forgiveness if we do it so lovingly as
he did in his time.   Forsooth every prayer offered up
of a penitent heart is acceptable unto our most good and
merciful Lord God, but that prayer above all other is
far more acceptable to Him which is approved by holy
Church and made by a man of marvellous and not unknown holiness: in the which prayer first is asked forgiveness of sins, strength of the soul to withstand sin, and
continuance of virtue. Which thing is nobly done in the
Psalms of David, namely in the VII Penitential Psalms.

---

[1] experienced.   [2] suitor.

whose declaration we have taken upon us. Therefore let
us gladly and lovingly recite[1] them, and oft offer them up
unto Almighty God, meekly asking forgiveness of Him
for our sins, which uncourteously we have committed and
done against His goodness.

In this part of the Psalm our prophet David doth
three things. First he calleth to mind his wretchedness.
Secondly he gathereth together many things whereby he
may trust for to have forgiveness. And thirdly he
sheweth that only by the help of Almighty God he continueth in this good purpose. Nothing that may be seen
or thought is more profitable whereby the mercy of God
may exercise and use His operation, than is our wretchedness, which in how much the more it be, so much more it
must move and stir our merciful Lord God to pity and
forgiveness. Therefore this prophet David, remembering it, calleth to mind all his offences and trespasses,
whereby he may shew his wretchedness to be great and
overheaped. He spake before of the inward parts of
misery; now he remembereth numbering the outward
parts of it. This prophet saith thus: " My wretchedness
standeth not only in the trouble of mine heart, which is
very great, nor in the feebleness of my strength, depressed
and put down by the tyranny of vices, neither in
the miserable blindness of my soul; but it is otherwise
increased, and by that whereof my chief comfort and
consolation ought to be had, which is a very unhappy
kind of wretchedness. Verily they that be my friends
and nigh about me, be mine adversaries and most against
me." Peradventure it should seem that we have said a
thing against reason to say that our friends and they that
be next us, be rather our enemies than our friends. But
and[2] we will call to mind and remember how much they
do let[3] us from getting the health of our souls, it should
to no man be a doubt. For what should be more precious and dearer unto us than time and long space of
life to do penance for our sins and trespasses done and
past, and to obtain many large rewards of God by doing
good works? Which goodness and good purpose is most

[1] The text has "desire."   [2] if.   [3] hinder.

of all taken away by them that be next about us and our friends,[1] namely that we call our friends. A certain doctor saith, "They be thieves and steal away our time of well-doing in this world." Also if we be in the will for to forsake this world or to take upon us a harder and a straiter way of living, who shall sooner withstand our good purpose than they which be as our friends and next about us? If we be in mind to sell all that we have and distribute it in alms unto the poor people, after the counsel of Christ, who will be more against us than our friends and neighbours? Oftentimes at great feasts, junkeries,[2] and drinkings we be made more intemperate and more disposed to vice than is convenient and honest for us to be. And by whose biddings and desires else, but by our friends and neighbours? Also of every word spoken unprofitably and in vain we shall give account before God: notwithstanding, it contenteth not our friends when we be in their company without we use many idle words and unfruitful both for body and soul. Moreover in whose causes and business doth our conscience more grudge and is hurt than in the causes and business of our neighbours and friends, when we help, defend or praise them to others, or else advance them ourself? And last, if our neighbours and friends see anything in us to be lauded or praised, they glaver[3] and praise it so much than anon we sin in vainglory, and also be proud of ourself. And if they spy anything in us that is lewd or to be forbidden, they will craftily colour it, or else go by as[4] they see it not, so that we never can know ourself. Wherefore they be to be thought rather our enemies than our friends. They seem to draw near us for our profit, but contrary they do against us and nothing for our profit. Our prophet saith in like manner *Amici mei et proximi mei adversum me appropinquaverunt et steterunt:* "My friends and neighbours drew nigh and stood stiffly against me." He speaketh not of them that be friends indeed (such be very scant, of whom it is written *Beatus qui invenit amicum verum:* "Blessed and happy is he that

---

[1] Probably this should read 'neighbours.'
[2] merrymakings.   [3] flatter.   [4] pretend.

F

hath found a true friend": peradventure at that time this prophet David had none such) but of the carnal and common friends whereof is a great number. He addeth saying *Et qui juxta me erant, de longe steterunt:* " They which were as my friends and my neighbours stood afar from me." Who shall we say is near any man if that his neighbour and friend be not? Who is to be thought more near than a neighbour or friend? Certainly none. But peradventure this prophet meant by 'them that be as neighbours and friends' such as favour and owe good will only to the body. And by 'those that be nigh unto us ' he meant them which have cure of souls. For they of very duty should first have the name of a friend and neighbour, for because the soul is next the body. And though it be so that every person hath charge of other in rebuking vices (According to the saying of our Saviour *Si peccaverit in te frater tuus, corripe eum:* " If thy brother (or even christian[1]) offend thee, correct him.") notwithstanding, the office of correction belongeth first unto prelates and unto such as hath cure of souls. Which be set in this world by Almighty God as overlookers of the people, unto whom is also commanded that they should shew to them their grievous offences; but they stand afar off, they spare to say the truth. Else let us go to the letter,[2] that is to say, bishops be absent from their dioceses and parsons from their churches; else[3] to the spiritual sense, as thus: no man will shew the filthiness of sins. All we use bypaths and circumlocutions in rebuking them. We go nothing nigh to the matter. And so in the mean season[4] the people perish with their sins. Which thing the prophet complaineth, saying *Et qui juxta me erant, de longe steterunt:* " They that had cure of my soul stood afar from me." Truly those be very wretches whom sins do subdue and put under the miserable yoke of servitude or bondage. They be also thrust down into a more straiter corner of misery when their friends and neighbours will not admonish and reprove their wickedness but suffer them so to continue;

[1] fellow-Christian.
[2] Either let us see if it be not literally so.   [3] or.   [4] while.

when also prelates and parsons do not correct their misliving and shortly call them to amendment, but rather
go by and suffer their mis-governance. What then?
Truly the soul, being glad of his destruction and in manner running on his own bridle, not helped by his friends,
nothing cared for of the bishops and such as hath cure
of souls, must needs come into the devil's power, which
as wood[1] enemies and ramping lions go about seeking
whom they may devour. They do the uttermost of their
power, they go sore to the matter,[2] and many times overcome such as be very strong. Therefore what marvel
is it if the devils catch the miserable soul, void and utterly destitute of all help, and so taken, draw it into
the deep pit of Hell? The prophet saith *Et vim jacie-
bant qui quærebant animam meam:* "They that sought
for to have my soul put great strength for to obtain their
purpose." The cursed devils' strength and power is very
great, as Scripture saith: *Non est potestas super terram
quæ comparetur eis:* "No strength upon the earth may be
compared to them." Which if they were suffered to
exercise upon mankind, none should be left alive. But
Almighty God of His goodness will not so suffer it; and
because of that, they give themself to frauds and guiles
studiously. Wherewith boldly they come unto us, per-
suading and shewing the vain pleasure of this world,
and the false joys of the flesh; wherewith they scorn
us daily, like as a man in his dream many times thinketh
to have great pleasures when no cause is so to be thought,
then waking he perceiveth himself deceived by his dream.
It is written: *Dormierunt somnium suum et nihil invener-
unt omnes viri divitiarum in manibus suis:* "Without
doubt sinners be beguiled, and all that they do be but
dreams and vanities." Which thing the prophet addeth,
saying *Et qui inquirebant mala mihi locuti sunt vanitates:*
"Such as were mine enemies and willed me rather evil
than good, spake and persuaded vanities unto me": that
is to say, worldly riches, pleasures and false fleshly joys.
And if it be so 'they may not take us by those vanities, 'then
they lay in our way other subtle and crafty baits; for

[1] mad.   [2] they are energetic.

their purpose is, either by continuance of one temptation or other, to make a man weary and cause him to think at the last that God will not help him, and so he falleth into despair. Either they be about[1] to bring a man to a higher perfection of life, to the end anon after they may overthrow him again, else they persuade and propose to a man's mind a more profitable place to get virtue in. Because why? They may likely or sooner put him down and make him forsake it; like as fishers do when they be about[1] to cause fish to come into their nets or other engines, they trouble the waters to make them avoid and flee from their wonted places. Sometime they persuade a man to change the manner of his life into a more strait way of living than peradventure any person may bear or suffer, that then he that is grieved[2] afterward give over and forsake it; like as men say apes be taken of the hunters by doing on shoes. For the property of an ape is to do as he seeth a man do. The hunter therefore will lay a pair of shoes in his way, and when he perceiveth the hunter doing on his shoes he will do the same; and so after that it is too hard for him to leap and climb from tree to tree as he was wont, but he falleth down, and anon is taken. Or else at some time they lay before a man venom privily hid under the colour of appearing virtue, as to set his mind on getting and to lay up worldly riches for the exercising of the works of mercy. Either[3] they move a man to chastise his body above his power from the sin of lechery. Thus by these frauds and other innumerable the devils be about to turn us from virtue, wherefore the prophet added *Et dolos tota die meditabantur:* "Daily their mind was to beguile me." But many times when we remember ourself to be tempted, we have so great pleasure in the thing shewed by suggestion, and it seemeth so joyful unto us, that we perceive no guile in it, or at the least we will not understand it. Therefore somewhat we hear and some we will not hear; we give audience only to it that soundeth to the voluptuous pleasures and profit of the body, and will not hear the privy guile hid under that bodily pleasure, but go by

---

[1] set themselves.　　[2] he finding it oppressive.　　[3] or else.

with a deaf ear. Which the prophet, in the person of us, sorroweth and waileth saying *Ego autem tanquam surdus non audiebam:* " I fared as a deaf man, would not hear the rebuking of worldly pleasure but gave heed to all that sounded pleasantly to the body." It were a great remedy to the sinner that is tempted, if he would diligently make privy search with himself of the thing laid unto his soul by suggestion, what may happen of it, whether good or evil. He may both ask question of himself, and make answer to the same; and anon, by that diligent Inquisition made, reason shall shew at the last if any peril be hid under by fraud or guile; and if none appear he may then flee unto Almighty God asking His help, which shall never be void or absent from any person that putteth his special trust in Him. But of a truth sinners oftentimes do the contrary; they make no search with themself, they ask not the help of Almighty God, but overthrow rather themself and in manner[1] the head downward; also, as dumb men, will nothing object or say against sin. Therefore it followeth *Et sicut mutus non aperiens os suum:* " I am as a dumb man not opening his mouth: I will not search and speak against mine own sin." St. James giveth monitions unto all such as feareth the devil's temptations, that they withstand strongly; and if they so do, the devil shall never after have boldness to let[2] and impugn them more. *Resistite diabolo et fugiet a vobis:* " Resist and withstand the devil and he shall flee from you." Which thing William Parisiense[3] confirmeth shewing of a certain person that against the foul and libidinous temptations of the flesh laid unto his soul by the devils, was wont to say with great indignation these words " Fie, fie, fie," and by this means he avoided those temptations. The Wise Man also counselleth us to hedge in our ears with thorns, saying: *Sæpi aures tuas spinis.* That is to say, ' If thou hear anything spoken that soundeth to evil or is not worthy to be spoken, as the devil's temptation, take thorns.' So much to say, ' withstand temptations sharply and bitterly.' Wherewith the devil shall be chased away from us. But

---

[1] as it were.   [2] hinder.   [3] See p. 34.

such as be overcome by temptations are very blind, not
perceiving the ugsomeness of sin; also they be deaf, not
hearing the fraud of the devil; and last they be dumb,
not speaking and wisely reproving the abomination of it.
So by custom they be made like unto dumb and deaf
persons utterly holding their peace. *Et factus sum sicut
homo non audiens et non habens in ore suo redargutiones:*
" I am made like unto a man that is deaf and dumb,
which neither will hear the rebuking of sin, nor say
against sin."

Hitherto our prophet hath described the miserable
and unhappy conditions of the sinner, expressing his
manifold wretchedness, which ye have heard. Now in
this second place he remembereth many things whereby
the goodness of God may be moved to forgiveness.
Among whom good hope is the first, without the which
everything that we do is of no value; for let us never
so much wail and sorrow our sins, confess them to never
so many priests and, lastly, study to purge them by as
much satisfaction as we can, all these profit nothing without hope. For was not Judas very penitent for his sins?
Yes, truly. For as Matthew saith: *Judas pœnitentia duc-
tus rettulit triginta argenteos principibus sacerdotum:*
" Judas, being penitent, brought again the thirty pence
to the princes of the priests," or " to the chief of the
Jews' Law." Did he not also shew openly his trespass
when he made exclamation and said *Peccavi tradens sanguinem justum:* " I have sinned grievously, betraying this
rightwise blood?" And lastly, he made satisfaction
more large than Almighty God would have asked. *Abiens
laqueo se suspendit:* " He went forth and hanged himself
in an halter." I beseech you, what more bitter and
shameful kind of satisfaction might have fortuned[1] him?
Verily none. And yet because he wanted hope and
despaired of forgiveness, all these did nothing profit him.
For, without doubt, desperation is so thick an obstacle
that, but if[2] it be taken away, the light of God's grace may
not come into our souls. Let us therefore take away the
obstacle of despair and open our souls by steadfast hope

---

[1] happened to.   [2] unless.

to receive the grace of God, and it must needs enter.
St. Paul saith *Deus negare seipsum non potest:* " Almighty God may not deny His own self." He cannot
but have mercy on wretched sinners that trust in Him.
He may no more withdraw from them the beams of His
grace, if their souls be made open by steadfast hope to
receive it, than the sun may withstand his beams out of
windows when they be open. Therefore the prophet saith
*Quoniam in te, Domine, speravi, tu exaudies me Domine
Deus meus:* " Blessed Lord, because I have trusted in
Thee, Thou shalt hear me, my Lord and my God." Of
a truth great and steadfast hope must needs alway be
heard. Notwithstanding, these few conditions following
must be joined to it: that is to say, if the thing asked of
Almighty God be belonging and not contrary to the soul's
health of the asker; also if he be willing and ready
to suffer correction for his sins; if he sorrow and wail
his error and be glad to accuse himself; lastly, if he will
beware and from that time forward abstain from all such
evil occasions. All these the prophet remembered by the
same order, and made his petition for to be heard, saying
Quoniam in te Domine speravi: " Lord, Thou shalt hear
me because I have trusted in Thee." He added the end
for the which he made his petition, that is to say, to the
intent his enemies have not the better of him, and be
much glad and joyful of his doing amiss. This prophet
neither asked earthly riches, worldly honours, pleasures
of the flesh, nor any other temporal thing, but only the
help of God's grace against his enemies that they joy
not much in his fall or hurt. Truly the devils be very
glad if at any season they may espy us waver or stumble
out of the way, breaking God's commandments. But
when we fall down and give place to the filthiness of sin,
not willing for to rise again, then they joy above
measure. Therefore this holy prophet rehearsed and
recited all these foresaid things because[1] Almighty God
should exercise His mercy, and soon help him, to the intent his enemies should not be glad at any time of his
fall to sin. *Quia dixi nequando supergaudeant mihi*

[1] in order that.

inimici mei: " Good Lord, I have recited all these and made my petition, because mine enemies at any time should not be very glad and merry of my fall in following the concupiscence of the body." These enemies lay a-wait both day and night, they spare us neither sleeping nor waking, eating or drinking, in labour, or any other study, but always busy themself to catch our souls in their snares. Almighty God with all the whole company of Heaven looketh down from above and beholdeth our trouble or agony that we have to withstand their malice and temptation; they also take it heavily and be sorry if we be overcome, and if we have the victory they be very glad and joyful. And on the other part these wicked devils doth espy and wait when we be about to fall down, and as soon as we set down our feet, and of a likelihood should slide or slip, then they make their vaunt of getting the victory, as it followeth: *Et dum commoventur pedes mei, super me magna locuti sunt:* " Whilst my feet were moved and about to slip," that is to say, " when my desires wavered and were removed from Almighty God, going unto sin, then mine enemies cracked[1] and spoke many great words joying and laughing me to scorn."

Furthermore he that will be heard of God must submit himself to wilful correction for his old sins, or at the least be ready in his soul to humble and submit himself. It is according with right and equity that the person which hath followed his own sensual pleasure against the will of Almighty God, redeem and make amends for his error, in[2] following the will of God, contrary to his own volupty and worldly pleasure. For sin must needs be punished either by our own self, or else by Almighty God. Which pain or punishment if that we take upon us with a good will, it is thought then we make satisfaction to Almighty God for our trespasses. We put this thing in execution and do it indeed, when we suffer patiently adversities and punishments of Almighty God, or injuries done by our neighbours,wilful[3] chastisements done by our own self, or else if we suffer patiently penance enjoined by our bishops or ghostly fathers after

[1] bragged.   [2] by.   [3] voluntary.

confession heard by them. All these be scourges whereby the noisomeness of sin is done away, the sinner
amended, and satisfaction is made to God. Wherefore
the prophet saith *Quoniam ego in flagella paratus sum*:
"I am ready, good Lord, to do all manner penance for my
sins," and not feignedly, but with a true and contrite
heart. But beside this manner of making satisfaction
is also asked, for a duty, of the sinner sorrow and inward repentance of the mind, for as much as he hath defiled the image of God within him, deserved eternal damnation, and lost the joy of Heaven. Because also he hath
so much displeased our best and most loving Lord God,
Which so dearly and so plenteously redeemed us with
the Precious Blood of His only begotten Son Jesus
Christ.

Alway the sinner must sorrow and wail, these
offences rehearsed, so oft as they come to his mind. We
find in Scripture that Peter, chief of all the Apostles,
wept and wailed daily his error in denying his Master
Christ Jesus. O how much unlike be these wretched
sinners unto Peter, that be glad when they have done
amiss and joy in their evil doings! Which thing truly
more displeaseth Almighty God than the sin done. It
is very hard at all times to remember and call to mind
that we have done amiss, and alway to sorrow; notwithstanding, this must at all seasons be firm and stable in
the soul, that as oft as the remembrance of sins cometh to
our minds so oft we must desire to be sorrowful for them.
And this we must do with all our power, strength, and
good will. For our penitent prophet said *Et dolor meus
in conspectu tuo semper*: "My sorrow for my sins was
always in the sight of mine understanding." Sorrow and
inward penance is not only[1] sufficient, but also we must
make confession, and shew to an able[2] priest our sins
when time shall require; else all our sorrow and penance,
be it never so grievous, shall be but in vain and of none
effect. In the which confession we may not tell fables
and other men's faults, but only our own; neither may
we shew our light sins, leaving the great and heavy un-

---

[1] alone.   [2] qualified.

shewed: we must also shew all our offences, small and great, without any shadow or colour, nothing excusing or making less, but express (as much as we may) the very wickedness with all the circumstance as it was done in deed. For this cause our penitent prophet added saying *Quoniam iniquitatem meam annuntiabo:* "Good Lord, I shall shew mine own wickedness or sin, even as it was, without colour or gloss." And lastly it is very necessary that we study and take heed in any wise never after to fall and turn again to sin, like a dog that turneth again to his vomit, or a sow once waltered[1] in the clay will return to that filthy place. That person which stedfastly hath purposed with himself to amend his life is always studious and busy to eschew and flee every occasion of sin, seeking wholesome remedies for the same. He remembered in himself how unwisely he fell, how short pleasure he had of it and soon done, also how long penance he is brought unto, continually to be permanent unto his life's end. He that can keep this thing alway present in the sight of his soul, remembering it inwardly, that person shall not likely return to his old sins. For this our prophet said *Et cogitabo pro peccato meo:* "I shall at all times remember and think on my sin," that nothing of it be uncontrite and unconfessed. Whosoever doeth all these things aforesaid, that is to say, he that asketh of Almighty God anything for his soul's health and do it with good hope, ready to correction, sorrowing his offences done, shewing truly the same by confession, and (last) purposing ever after to abstain from all occasions of sin, without doubt that person shall be heard and obtain his petition.

Yet is behind[2] to be spoken of which we said in the third place: how this prophet shewed that he might not continue in goodness without the help of God. That person which of long season hath had in experience, and customably used himself in exercising, guile and frauds, may lightly compass a simple and unwise creature and bring him out of the way whither he list. Now if there be many such, and all they with one assent enviously

---

[1] wallowed.   [2] remains.

have conspired the death of a simple person, how may he flee so great malice and namely[1] so much put in exercise?[2] Truly it is a thing incredible. It may not be done, without some man more mighty than they withstand and defend him. We all be in like case. There is none of us but some wicked spirit pursueth him with great hatred; and surely this wicked spirit by long and daily exercise hath gotten by craft a thousand wiles and means to beguile any person. For from the beginning of the world unto this time being alive, he hath learnt all deceitful crafts whereby any man may be subverted, be he never so strong. And moreover whensoever he hath gotten the better of any person, he is by that deed made the bolder and in manner more strong; and he that is so overcome is made the weaker and more feeble. Therefore this prophet saith in the person of us all *Inimici autem mei vivunt et confirmati sunt super me:* " Mine enemies be alive and have strength far above me." I may well say they be alive. For why? They are immortal. They be far stronger than we be, for by often having the victory they have taken upon them more boldness. If at any time a sinner flee to holy penance purposing to amend his life and diligently purge his conscience with weeping tears, and so chase away the wicked spirit that impugneth him, yet he is not clean delivered; for the same evil spirit will anon come again and bringeth with him seven others more wicked than himself, and by new frauds is about craftily to subdue that person. Which our Saviour affirmeth in the Gospel of Luke, and the prophet in this place waileth the same, saying *Et multiplicati sunt qui oderunt me inique:* " Those that wickedly and of very malice did hate me be multiplied, they be increased to a more number." Not only damned spirits be malicious adversaries to me but also their helpers, that is to say perverse and cursed folks to whom everything well done is odious or hateful. Namely when they see any person that hath despised wicked conversation, worldly glosses or flatterings, and by holy penance is become a new man, then these ministers of

---

[1] especially.   [2] so well trained.

the devil and furtherers of his malice, more loving darkness than light, like unto a beast called a back,[1] do backbite, pursue and laugh him to scorn; whereas they should
praise and give thanks unto such penitent persons. For
the more that are penitent, the more prayers in number
and more acceptable be offered up to Almighty God;
wherewith He being pleased deferreth His grievous
punishment and shortly doth not shew vengeance upon
sinners, which daily do provoke His goodness to their
utter undoing. These wicked sinners therefore be very
unkind and much set against them that be converted into
a better life by penance. And, as the prophet saith, they
give and reward evil for good. *Qui retribuunt mala
pro bonis detrahebant mihi, quoniam sequebar bonita-
tem:* " Such as give in reward evil for good did malici-
ously backbite me because I followed goodness." Our
Saviour said to His Apostles *Si de mundo fuissetis, mundus quod suum est diligeret. Sed quia de mundo non
estis, propterea odit vos mundus:* " If ye were of the
world, the world should love you. But because ye be
not of the world, therefore it hateth you." They that
take upon them the way of penance doth forsake worldly
conversation and in no wise be conformed to it: for the
which they be forsaken of the world. What shall we
do? The devil many times grieveth us, the world pursueth and followeth us, what remedy may be gotten
amongst so many adversaries? Truly He that is
Almighty may succour us and none other. Let us busily
ask His help, for since our adversaries continually every
moment do pursue us, therefore we must pray continually
unto Almighty God. Which our Saviour confirmeth saying *Oportet semper orare:* " We must always pray." If
the help of His grace be not ready at all seasons we
must needs sag and bow. Therefore like as our prophet,
according to the manner of a sick man that is in great
peril and sore vexed with sickness will that the physician
forsake him not in any manner wise, neither go from him
at any season, but diligently give heed to make him
whole: so our prophet prayeth unto Almighty God that

---

[1] bat.

He forsake him not, neither go from him at any time
but give heed unto his help. Let us all do in like wise,
saying with the prophet *Ne derelinquas me, Domine
Deus: ne discesseris a me. Intende in adjutorium meum:*
" Blessed Lord God, forsake us not, go not away from
us but give heed unto our help." The voice of the cursed
devils when they see a man in their power and in manner
forsaken of God is this, they say *Deus dereliquit eum:
persequimini et comprehendite eum: quia non est qui
eripiat:* " God hath forsaken him, let us pursue and catch
him, for he is without help, none can deliver him." Truly
if we be forsaken of Almighty God, none else can deliver us from the power of them.   And contrariwise, if
God be present and with us, our adversaries dare not
meddle in any condition.[1] It is written *Si Deus nobiscum,
quis contra nos?* " If Almighty God be with us, who may
say or do against us?" Therefore let us all say *Ne derelinquas me, Domine Deus meus:* " Good Lord, forsake
us not." Moreover if Almighty God go from us at any
time, our enemies suddenly will come upon us by subtle
craft and shortly have the better, without we be soon
helped.   For this let us all say with the prophet, that
followeth: *Ne discesseris a me:* " Blessed Lord, go not
from me." Holy Fathers say that Almighty God will
sometime withdraw His presence that the devils may
have interest and licence to tempt a man, for because[2]
his victory and reward for the same should be the more,
if that he resist and right strongly withstand their unhappy temptations. Which thing done we read of holy
St. Anthony, that after his sharp and grievous beatings
he said unto God at His coming again to him: " Ah, my
Lord, where hast Thou been; where art Thou, good
Jesus?" And our Lord said unto him: " Anthony, I was
here with thee; notwithstanding, I tarried to see thy battle, and forasmuch as thou hast so manfully withstood
and gave no place to thine adversaries in fighting against
them, I shall alway help and succour thee." For this
the prophet saith *Intende in adjutorium meum, Domine
Deus salutis meæ:* " My Lord and God of mine health,

---

[1] wise.   [2] in order that.

give heed to mine help." Cassianus saith, " These words be of great virtue and always to be had in remembrance." Which also the Church useth very often in the service of God, at all times asketh His help in the beginning of it. Let us therefore, which be wrapped and closed in all these miseries afore rehearsed, go by prayer unto our best and merciful Lord God, with steadfast hope and true penance, and meekly beseech Him of His help, that since He only may defend us from our enemies, will vouchsafe to deliver us from them, also not to go away neither forsake us, but always give heed unto our help. *Quoniam ipse est Dominus Deus salutis nostræ.* For why? " He is God and Lord of our health," giving temporal health to our bodies, and to our souls the health of grace in this life, and in the general resurrection to come (which we verily trust) everlasting health both to body and soul. To the which our Lord by His ineffable mercy bring us. Amen.

THE FOURTH PENITENTIAL PSALM.
MISERERE MEI DEUS.
PSALM 1 (Part I)

THAT man were put in great peril and jeopardy that should hang over a very deep pit, holden up by a weak and slender cord or line, in whose bottom be most wood[1] and cruel beasts of every kind, abiding with great desire his falling down, for that intent, when he shall fall down, anon to devour him; which line or cord that he hangeth by, should be holden up and stayed only by the hands of that man to whom by his manifold ungentleness he hath ordered and made himself as a very enemy. Likewise, dear friends, consider in yourself. If now under me were such a very deep pit, wherein might be lions, tigers, and bears gaping with open mouth to destroy and devour me at my falling down, and that there be nothing whereby I might be holden up and succoured but a broken bucket or

---

[1] furious.

pail which should hang by a small cord, stayed and hold-
en up only by the hands of him, to whom I have behaved
myself as an enemy and adversary by great and grievous
injuries and wrongs done unto him, would ye not think me
in perilous conditions? Yes, without fail. Truly all we
be in like manner. For under us is the horrible and
fearful pit of Hell, where the black devils in the likeness
of ramping and cruel beasts doth abide desirously our
falling down to them. The lion, the tiger, the bear, or
any other wild beast never layeth so busily a-wait for
his prey when he is hungry, as doth these great and horrible hell-hounds, the devils, for us. Of whom may be
heard the saying of Moses: *Dentes bestiarum immittam
in eos cum furore trahentium atque serpentum:* " I shall
send down amongst them wild beasts to gnaw their flesh,
with the woodness[1] of cruel birds and serpents drawing
and tearing their bones." There is none of us living but
that is holden up from falling down to Hell in as feeble
and frail vessel, hanging by as weak line as may be. I
beseech you, what vessel may be more bruckle[2] and frail
than is our body that daily needeth reparation, and if
thou refresh it not, anon it perisheth and cometh to
nought? A house made of clay, if it be not often renewed and repaired with putting to of new clay, shall at
the last fall down. And much more this house made of
flesh, this house of our soul, this vessel wherein our soul
is holden up and borne about, but if[3] it be refreshed by
often feeding and putting to of meat and drink, within
the space of three days it shall waste and slip away. We
be daily taught by experience how feeble and frail man's
body is; also beholding daily the goodly and strong
bodies of young people, how soon they die by a short
sickness. And therefore Solomon in the book called
Ecclesiasticus compareth the body of man to a pot that is
brocle,[2] saying *Memento Creatoris tui in diebus juventu-
tis tuæ, antequam conteratur hydria super fontem:* "Have
mind on thy Creator and Maker in the time of thy young
age, ere ever the pot be broken upon the fountain ": that
is to say, thy body, and thou peradventure fall into the

---

[1] fury.　　[2] brittle.　　[3] unless.

well; that is to say, into the deepness of Hell. This pot (man's body) hangeth by a very weak cord, which the said Solomon in the same place calleth a cord or line made of silver: *Et antequam rumpatur funiculus argenteus:* " Take heed by faith, ere the silver cord be broken." Truly this silver cord whereby our soul hangeth and is holden up in this pot, in this frail vessel, our body, is the life of man. For as a little cord or line is made or woven of a few threads, so is the life of man knit together by four humours, that as long as they be knit together in a right order so long is man's life whole and sound. This cord also hangeth by the hands and power of God. For as Job saith: *Quoniam in illius manu est anima (id est vita) omnis viventis:* " In His hand and power is the life of every living creature." And we by our unkindness done against His goodness have so greatly provoked Him to wrath that it is a marvel this line be so long holden up by His power and majesty; and if it be broken, this pot our body is broken, and the soul slippeth down into the pit of Hell, there to be torn and all-to-rent of[1] those most cruel hell-hounds. O, good Lord, how fearful condition stand we in, if we remember these jeopardies and perils! And if we do not remember them, we may say, O marvellous blindness, yea our madness, never enough to be wailed and cried out upon! Heaven is above us, wherein Almighty God is resident and abiding, Which giveth Himself to us as our Father, if we obey and do according unto His holy commandments. The deepness of Hell is under us, greatly to be abhorred, full of devils. Our sins and wickedness be afore us. Behind us be the times and spaces that were offered to do satisfactions and penance, which we have negligently lost. On our right hand be all the benefits of our most good and meek Lord Almighty God given unto us. And on our left hand be innumerable misfortunes that might have happened if that Almighty God had not defended us by His goodness and meekness. Within us is the most stinking abomination of our sin, whereby the image of Almighty God within us is very foul deformed, and by that

[1] torn to pieces by.

we be made unto Him very enemies. By all these things
before rehearsed we have provoked the dreadful majesty
of Him unto so great wrath that we must needs fear,
lest that He let fall this line from His hands, and the pot
our body be broken, and we then fall down into the deep
dungeon of Hell.   Therefore what shall we wretched
sinners do?   Of whom may help and succour be had and
obtained for us?   By what manner sacrifice may the
wrath and ire of so great a Majesty be pacified and made
easy?   Truly the best remedy is to be swift in doing
penance for our sins.   He only may help them that be
penitent. By that only sacrifice His ire is mitigate and
assuaged chiefly. Our most gracious Lord Almighty God
is merciful to them that be penitent.   Therefore let us
now ask His mercy with the penitent prophet David. Let
us call and cry before the throne of His grace, saying
Miserere mei Deus: " God have mercy on me."
    First let us teach a part of this Psalm, as we did be-
fore in the other Psalms. We shall at this time by the
help of Almighty God declare the half of it. Wherein
our prophet doth three things. First he induceth and
bringeth in his petition, which every penitent person may
make apt and convenient to himself. After that, he
sheweth by many reasons his petitions to be granted. And
lastly he promiseth very true and undoubtful hope to
himself of the desire that he asketh. If that sinners
would truly and rightfully ponder and think of what condition and state they be in (of the which somewhat we
have said before) I trow they should think themself
in a very great peril and jeopardy. And if that they remember it not well, truly the more is their peril and
great jeopardy. For, of the two, that person is more nigh
the health of his soul that seeth and perceiveth before
the danger or peril that he may fall into, than is he that
hath no mind upon it.   For he that casteth[1] no peril
before may not flee the chance when it shall happen.
We therefore knowing the perilous condition we be in,
let us seek a remedy for to avoid it. Which can nowhere
else be had but only of Almighty God: *Nam quis potest*

---

[1] forecasteth.

G

dimittere peccata nisi solus Deus? " For who may else forgive sins but only our Blessed Lord Almighty God?" Let us all therefore cry unto Him, saying *Miserere mei Deus:* " God, have mercy on me." Peradventure some man will think in himself : if no remedy may be else had but of Almighty God, Whose majesty I, ungracious sinner, have so oft and so grievously offended, heaping sin upon sin, how shall He so lightly have mercy upon me? How may it be that He shall not take vengeance and punish me, since He is so mighty and rightwise? For great men in power of this world, the more mighty and rightwise they be, so much the more they exercise and use vengeance and punishment upon them that be wicked and breakers of the law. Therefore sith Almighty God is most rightwise and most mighty of all, how may He have mercy and not avenge His quarrel of so many and great trespasses done against His highness? Unto this we answer in this manner wise : that the judges of this world (if any be without falseness and malice) be so obedient and subject unto the laws, which alway they must obey, that it is not lawful to them at their own will and arbitrament to forgive such as shall please them. Also many of them (and almost all) have so much cursedness and malice set in their minds that, if that they might, they will not forgive those that hath offended them in any condition. For why? They have but little mercy and almost none. It is written *Nemo bonus nisi solus Deus:* " No man is good but only Almighty God." He only is of so great meekness and pity that no point of malice neither of falseness may be in Him. Therefore since He is so meek and so merciful, and above His laws, also in no condition subject to them, He may forgive and be merciful to whom He will ; and so shall He do, for He may not have little mercy but always great and plenteous. Truly the mercy of our most mighty and best Lord is great, and so great that it hath all measure of greatness. Sometimes trees be called great for their goodly and large height. Pits be called great for their deepness. Far journeys be called great because they are long. Streets and highways be called great for their breadth and wideness. But the mercy of God containeth and is measured by all these measures of greatness, and not only by one of them. Of the greatness in height is written *Domine, usque ad cœlos misericordia tua:* " Lord Thy mercy extendeth and reacheth up to the heavens." It is also great in deepness, for it reacheth down to the lowest Hell. The prophet saith *Misericordia tua magna est super me: et eruisti animam meam ex inferno inferiori:* " Lord, Thy mercy is great over me, and Thou hast delivered me from the lowest and deepest Hell." It is broad, for it occupieth and overcovereth all the world, the same prophet saying *Misericordia Domini plena est terra:* " The earth is full of the mercy of our Lord." It lacketh no length, for also it is spoken of the same prophet *Misericordia ejus ab æterno et usque in æternum super timentes eum:* " The mercy of God is without end on them that dreadeth Him." Therefore sith the mercy of God is so high, so deep, so broad and so long, who can or may say or think it little? Who shall not call it great by all measures of greatness? Then every creature that will acknowledge himself to this mercy may say *Miserere mei, Deus, secundum magnam misericordiam tuam:* " Lord have mercy on me according to Thy great mercy." Two things there be concerning mercy: that is to say, inward mercy, and the work of mercy outwardly done. There lieth peradventure in the open street a poor man full of sores: a certain physician coming by beholdeth him and is moved anon with inward pity ; nevertheless, he goeth beside[1] and giveth him no medicine at all. Truly although this physician were somewhat merciful to this poor man, yet he shewed no deed of mercy unto him. And we ourself oftentimes see and behold many needy and sick folks, unto whom we give no help, albeit we be somewhat moved inwardly with pity and mercy. Our prophet therefore saith of very right in another place, praising the mercy of God, *Misericors et miserator Dominus.* He is ' *misericors* ' that is moved with some mercy inwardly. ' *Miserator* ' is he that doeth and performeth outwardly the deed of mercy. Therefore our Lord is not only mer-

---

[1] by.

ciful inwardly, but also He exerciseth outwardly the work
of it. And if He executed not mercy in deed, what
should it profit us? For why? We shall feel no remedy,
by inward pity only, of the grievousness that we suffer,
and before were overthrown by, without the deed of
mercy be shewed. It is not therefore enough that Almighty God have mercy on us but if[1] He do the deed of
mercy. And what other thing is to give and shew on us
the work of mercy but to do away our wretchedness, that
is to say, our sins whereby we be made wretched? Scripture saith *Miseros facit populos peccatum:* " Sin maketh
wretched people." It is very needful truly to pray that
Almighty God be merciful unto us and also vouchsafe to
execute the deed of His mercy on us, that is to say, to
do away our sins and give us His mercy according to the
multitude of His mercies. If thou sin once, it is needful to thee one mercy, whereby that sin may be done
away. If twice or thrice or peradventure more often,
then it shall be needful to thee so many mercies as thy
sins be. Of a truth the mercies of Almighty God be innumerable. For like as from the great light of the sun
cometh and sheweth forth innumerable beams, so from
the great mercy of Almighty God goeth forth innumerable mercies. Number the sunbeams if it be possible,
and the mercies of Almighty God be more without end.
How grievous and how great soever our sin be, yet the
mercy of God is much more, whereby He may be merciful to us. And how many soever they be in number, yet
the mercies of Him be many more, by the which He may
do away all our trespasses. Therefore with great confidence and trust let us ask of Him His mercy, saying
*Et secundum multitudinem miserationum tuarum dele
iniquitatem meam:* " Good Lord, do away my sin, according to the multitude of Thy mercies." If a table
be foul and filthy of a long continuance, first we rasé it,
after when it is rased we wash it, and last after the washing we wipe and make it clean. A soul is compared unto
a table whereon nothing was painted, nevertheless with
many misdoings and spots of sin we have defiled and

[1] unless.

made it deformed in the sight of God. Therefore it is needful that it be rased, washed and wiped. It shall be rased by the inward sorrow and compunction of the heart when we be sorry for our sin. It shall be washed with the tears of our eyes when we acknowledge and confess our sin. And lastly it shall be wiped and made clean when that we be about[1] for to make amends and do satisfaction by good deeds for our sins.

These three things that we have spoken of cometh without doubt of the gracious pity of God. Thou art sorry for thy sin? It is a gift of Almighty God. Thou makest knowledge[2] of thy sin, weeping and wailing for it? It is a gift of Almighty God. Thou art busy in good works to do satisfaction? Which also is a gift of Almighty God. We have asked now of Almighty God that He do away our sins by rasing of our soul, that is contrition; let us again ask and desire Him to wash us from the same, that is to say, He grant and give us grace to weep and wail for it. We weep sometime, but it cometh not of God. As when we suffer adversities against our will: when our weeping tears doth profit us nothing, but rather doth hurt. For St. Paul saith *Sæculi tristitia mortem operatur:* "The sorrow of this world for loss of worldly pleasures and desires causeth everlasting death." Such sorrows and weepings washeth not the soul, but rather make it foul. Other weeping tears there be that be caused of the sorrow which is godly, as when we be sorrowful that we have so much displeased God Who hath done so much for us. *Hæc tristitia pænitentiam in salutem stabilem operatur:* "This sorrow (as saith St. Paul) causeth penance to be had, for everlasting health." And as saith St. Chrysostom: *Hæ lachrimæ lavant delictum:* "These weeping tears wash away sin." They be also given of the Holy Ghost to them that be penitent. For it is written *Flabit spiritus ejus et fluent aquæ:* "The spirit of God shall give so great infusion of grace to them that be penitent that the waters (that is to say, their weeping tears) shall flow and be abundant." Upon these waters the spirit of Almighty God may fly and

---

[1] set ourselves.   [2] acknowledgment.

go swiftly: which was figured in the beginning of Scripture, by the saying of Moses *Et Spiritus Domini ferebatur
super aquas:* " The spirit of our Lord was borne aloft
upon the waters." Chrysostom describeth the virtue of
these weeping tears, saying *Sicut post vehementes imbres
mundus aer ac purus efficitur: ita et post lachrimarum
pluvias serenitas mentis sequitur atque tranquillitas:*
" Like as after great showers and storms the air is made
clean and pure, so after great plenty of weeping tears
followeth the clearness and tranquillity of the soul."
Let us all therefore desire and ask to be washed from
our sins by these waters, and say unto Almighty God *Am-
plius lava me ab iniquitate mea:* " Lord, wash me more
from my wickedness." Beside rasing of our soul (that
is, contrition) and washing (that is, confession) we said
that it is necessary to be wiped and made clean. Which
is done by satisfaction of good works. First by almsdeeds and charitable distribution to the poor people. For
our Saviour said *Date eleemosynam, et ecce omnia munda
sunt vobis:* " Give alms, and ye shall be made clean from
all sin." By almsdeeds therefore and good works we
may be wiped and made clean from all sin. And no
creature of himself hath power to do good works without
the grace and help of God. For as saith St. Paul *Non
sumus sufficientes cogitare aliquid ex nobis, quasi ex nobis, sed sufficientia nostra ex Deo est:* " We be not sufficient and able of ourself, as of ourself, to think any
manner thing, but our sufficiency and ability dependeth
and cometh of God only." Therefore this thing is to
be asked of God that He vouchsafe to move our souls
perfectly by His grace unto the exercising and doing of
many good works, that they may be utterly wiped and
made clean from all contagions of sin, according to the
desire and saying of the prophet that followeth: *Et a
peccato meo munda me:* " Good Lord, make me clean
from my sin." Our whole petition is ended here, wherein
first we have asked that God be merciful unto us after
His great mercy; and that He rase our souls, wash them
and wipe them utterly from all sin, according to the multitude of His manifold mercies.

In this second member be divers strong reasons brought forth, whereby God may be moved so that He may not deny our petition. Three things we have asked before. First that God do away our sin by contrition, wash our soul by confession, and thirdly make it clean by satisfaction. To the which other three, correspondent to them, be brought forth and shewed in this first syllogism (in this first reason) although they be not in the same order. To do away sin (as we said) is to rase it, that no spot be seen in our soul, in like manner as letters be done away when they be rased, so that nothing which was there written may be read or known. Truly Almighty God will not know our sin and trespass, if we ourself will know them. If we study and be about (as our duty is) to read and consider the sins that be written and marked in our souls, anon He of His goodness putteth them out of His sight. Therefore let us all say with a contrite heart and mind, " O Blessed Lord God do away my sin and wickedness ": *Quoniam iniquitatem meam ego cognosco:* " For I know my great and grievous trespass." It is greatly acceptable in the sight of our most merciful Lord God if a sinner will call to mind with due contrition and greatness of his sin; also Whom he hath offended and how grievously; into how many hurts and things unprofitable he hath fallen for his sin; and how many profits he hath lost by the reason of it. If we were in mind busily to behold and look on these things it should be to us right profitable. For why? An[1] we know our sins after this manner, anon God forgiveth and doth them away. And the more often we do, the sooner He forgetteth. If we call to mind unfeignedly and without any dissimulation how much our sins doth hinder and let us from doing good works, that blessed Lord shall utterly forget and do them away for ever, so that one little spot shall not also be left, but in every part to appear fair and clean. Let us therefore with contrition say also this that followeth, " Lord make me clean from my sin ": *Quoniam peccatum meum contra me est semper:* " For my sin is always against me." How

---

[1] if.

against me? Truly even directly before my eyes that I may behold and look upon it at all times without any let.[1] Now we have spoken of the doing away of our sin, and making clean of our soul, and also why God should so do; let us now also shew why He should wash it, to the intent every particle that we have promised to speak of may answer conveniently to other. The weeping tears whereby our souls may be washed, cometh of a special gift of God, and namely[2] when we have that grace to weep in confession and acknowledging our sins before His fearful Highness, knowing also the grievousness of it, we shall soon know the greatness of our sin. First, if we will consider well how great and mighty Lord He is Whom we have offended. Another,[3] if we take good heed how much our ungentleness hath been to Him, looking on us, when we do so many and great offences. God only is of that power that if we offend and trespass against His goodness we be guilty to suffer eternal death for it. David offended grievously against Uriah his knight, whom he caused to be slain. And also he did wickedly to Bersabe, wife to the said Uriah, which he persuaded to adultery. Nevertheless if he had not broken the law and commandment of God by the said offences, he had not been guilty and worthy of eternal death. Therefore of a truth none offence may be done to any creature whereof the doer should stand in the jeopardy of eternal death, but only for offending against Almighty God. Whom we offend much more grievously that He beholdeth and seeth every trespass that we do, be they little, be they much. Therefore let us all go by prayer unto Almighty God, saying, " O my Lord God, behold and see. I, wretched sinner, acknowledge and confess my guilt before Thy Majesty; before Thy sight I detect my trespass, I do not hide it; I shew forth my sin to be very grievous. But, Blessed Lord, I beseech Thee wash me with my weeping tears, coming out from the plenteousness of Thy grace. And furthermore wash me from my sin. For why? Good Lord, I acknowledge *Quod tibi soli peccavi:* " That only to Thee I have tres-

---

[1] hindrance.   [2] especially.   [3] another way to know it is.

passed and offended before Thy sight." For this cause,
good Lord, forgive and do away my sin. For why?   I
know my trespass, I know well I have offended Thee.
And besides that, wash me; for I myself confess that
only to Thee I have offended. And so, in conclusion,
make me clean because my sin is as an object to my sight,
it is ever in my sight. Blessed Lord, if Thy Highness
may not by these reasons be moved to mercy, yet let this
move and stir Thee to be merciful: *Ut justificeris in sermonibus tuis:* that is to say, " that thou mayst be justified in Thy words and sayings." It is written by thine
holy prophet Ezechiel, what judgments universal Thou
gave unto the people. Thou sayest also, good Lord: *Nolo
mortem impii, sed ut convertatur impius a via sua et
vivat:* " I will not the death of a sinner, but that he be
turned from his wicked life and live." Thou sayest also:
*Impietas impii non nocebit ei in quacunque die conversus
fuerit ab impietate sua:* " The misliving, the wickedness,
of the sinful creature shall never hurt neither be noisome
to him whensoever he will turn from his wickedness."
And again Thou sayest: *Si egerit pœnitentiam a peccato
suo, vita vivet et non morietur; omnia peccata ejus que
peccavit non imputabuntur ei:* " If a sinner do penance
for his sin, he shall live and never die everlastingly; the
sins and trespasses that he hath done shall never be cast
in his teeth, neither laid to his charge." O Blessed Lord,
vouchsafe and give us leave to ask Thee this question.
Were not these Thy words, did Thou not speak them
to Thy prophet, or did he beguile us that said they were
spoken of Thee? For of a truth he wrote that Thou
spake them to him: *Tu itaque, fili hominis, dic ad filios
populi tui:* " Thou, the son of a man, shew and tell this
unto thy people, &c." Therefore, Good Lord, they be
Thy words. O most meek God, behold, we wretched
sinners turn from our evil ways unto Thee, we do penance
for our offences ; grant, Lord, that they be not noisome
to us neither laid to our charge at any time, but utterly
to be done away, washed away and wiped away. *Ut
justificeris in sermonibus tuis:* " That Thou may be justified by Thy words." Thou knowest well what foolhardy

judgment the people gave against Thee for this Thy sentence: they said *Non est æqua via Domini:* " The way that this Man taketh is not equal." The people presumed to be judges of Thy sentence. To whom Thou gave answer on this wise: *Numquid via mea non est æqua, et non magis viæ vestræ pravæ sunt?* " Is not My way good and equal, and yours shrewd, nought, and more unequal?" Thou confirmed again to them Thy words spoken before, saying *Quando averterit se impius ab impietate sua feceritque judicium et justitiam, vita vivet et non morietur; omnium iniquitatum ejus quas operatus est non recordabor:* " Whensoever a sinner shall turn away from his sin and truly confess him of it and make satisfaction, he shall live and never die everlastingly. I shall also forget and never call to mind any sin that he hath done." Good Lord, Thy will was to overcome and exclude by this manner their foolhardy judgment against Thy merciful sentence. We beseech and pray Thee now to do the same. Thou shalt not overcome their opinions but if Thou manifest and shew Thy words and sayings to be true and that they have untruly judged of Thee. Therefore now, Blessed Lord, do away our wickedness, now forget our sins which we utterly forsake and despise. *Ut justificeris in sermonibus tuis et vincas cum judicaris:* " That Thou may be justified in Thy words, and overcome when Thou art judged so boldly and foolishly." Our sins be great and innumerable; we do not forget them, we do not cover and hide them, we do not defend them, but we know, we make open and accuse them; nevertheless we beseech Thee for Thy great mercy and for the infinite multitude of Thy manifold mercies, behold us; and namely, whereof we be made, Thou knowest what matter it is and how frail it is. Call again to mind that we are but dust and clay, and also that the law and custom of our body is contrary to the law and custom of our soul, and the custom of our body putteth us daily under the captivity and thraldom of sin. If a commandment were given to a man that hath but a weak and feeble body in strength, to roll and turn up a millstone of a great weight unto the highest part of a hill, and that he put his good will to perform the same; nevertheless, peradventure whilst he is about to do the deed, the stone for greatness of his weight above his strength falleth down backward into a valley. Were not this man more worthy to be pardoned and forgiven (seeing and knowing his good mind) than he that were mighty and hath great strength? We be in like condition, we be about to bring this our body unto Thy holy hill; nevertheless it is thrust down by the heavy burden of sin, that oftentimes it boweth and slippeth down backward. For that same sin that by our first father and mother, Adam and Eve, was brought amongst all men is heavy and grievous on us like as an heavy burden, and daily grieveth us more and more; it maketh us also prone and ready to all other vices. Therefore and for this cause have mercy on us, for this sin of our forefather, this heavy and grievous weight, was conceived and begotten with us, according to the saying of the prophet *Ecce enim in iniquitatibus conceptus sum et in peccatis concepit me mater mea:* " Behold I was conceived in sin, and my mother conceived me in sin." This notwithstanding, good Lord, we know that Thou art true, and all that Thou dost promise is very truth. Truly Thou said that Thy coming into this world was to call sinners to penance. *Non veni vocare justos sed peccatores ad pœnitentiam:* (this is Thy saying) " I came into this world, not to call rightwise people, but sinners to penance." Thou hast called on them and daily dost call, saying, *Venite ad me omnes qui laboratis et onerati estis et ego reficiam vos:* " All ye that labour in this world and bear heavy, by doing penance come to Me and I shall refresh you." Truly Thy promise is to receive all that will come, if they come to Thee as they should do. *Qui venit ad me non ejiciam foras:* " Whosoever cometh to Me I shall not cast him out, I shall not forsake him." O good Lord, behold, we be sinners in like manner as Thou came into the world to call unto Thee, we labour and be laden with the multitude of our sins, we also be made weary by the means of our wickedness. Therefore, blessed Lord, say unto us, " Come ye unto Me," and anon we

come, we humble and meek ourself before the throne
of Thy mercy. Other hope and trust have we none in
any condition but only in Thee. If Thou wilt not be
merciful to us for accusing ourself, neither by this that
Thou art justified by Thy words, neither also for our
frailty, yet, good Lord, have mercy on us for Thy truth.
Thou art true and lovest truth above all things. Have
in mind the promise Thou made to every penitent sinner
coming unto Thee, which is, Thou shalt not cast them
away, and also Thou shalt refresh them. We come therefore unto Thee, good Lord, cast us not away, but refresh
us with thy grace and mercy. *Ecce enim veritatem dil-
existi:* " Thou hast ever loved truth."

After that this holy prophet hath shewed and purposed his petition, and brought forth many reasons why
the said petition should be granted; thirdly now with a
glad cheer he maketh sure promise and hope to himself
to get and obtain his asking, willing to give example to
every sinner because that they should do the same. It
is a great difference between despair and sure hope. The
Ninivites, when the prophet threatened and menaced
them with the destruction of the city, they were not in
surety God would be merciful to them, neither they were
utterly in despair. Jonas the prophet came unto them
the second time, sent from Almighty God, and said
openly *Adhuc quadraginta dies et Ninive subvertetur:*
" Within forty days to come the city of Ninive shall be
overthrown and destroyed." The people hearing the
words of the prophet Jonas and fearing the vengeance of
God to fall upon them, commanded among themself
every man, woman and child to fast, and also clad them
in sackcloth from the lowest degree unto the highest,
The king of that city, anon as he was certified and had
knowledge of the prophet's saying, rose up from his seat,
threw away his royal garment and clad him in sackcloth,
and sat down on the ground in the dust; and, by the de-
cree and one assent of all his nobles, commanded that
every man, woman and child, and also brute beasts,
should not eat, neither drink, by a certain space, but
that everybody should do penance for their sin. This

was their saying: *Quis scit si convertatur et ignoscat Deus et revertatur a furore iræ suæ et non peribimus?* " Who knoweth, who is sure, if God will be turned from vengeance and by His mercy forgive us, and also withdraw His wrath and we shall not perish?" It appeareth by these words they had no very trust of forgiveness and also that they were not utterly in despair; notwithstanding, they did penance, abiding all together what the most meek God would do with them. Whose great mercy at the last they knew and had in experience, although before they neither had very trust nor full mistrust of it. But we be now in another condition. Almighty God hath shewed to us Christian people the treasures of His great mercy, the secret mysteries of the Faith and the Sacraments of health, whereby we may trust verily to have forgiveness. Certainly they were before hid and unknown to us, but now of late time they be manifest and shewed by His only begotten Son, Jesus Christ, Which His own self doth witness, saying unto His Father *Abscondisti hæc a sapientibus et revelasti ea parvulis:* " Father, Thou hast hid and kept secret the privities of Thy Godhead from wise and cunning men and shewed them to such as be small and of little reputation in this world." Jesu Christ, coming down from the Father of Heaven into this world, made open and shewed unto His Church the hid and privy mysteries of His Godhead; His own self beareth witness, saying: *Quæcumque audivi a patre meo, nota feci vobis:* " I have manifested and shewed to you all that I have heard of My Father." He promised also at His Ascension the Holy Ghost to come, that should teach perfectly the knowledge of everything. So that now nothing may be more certain to us than it which is taught by Holy Church. No means may be found so speedful and ready to prove the certainty of anything concerning our faith as that the Church hath so affirmed and ordained. The Church of God may in no wise beguile in those things that belongeth to our faith and to the undoubtful health of the soul. Who therefore of us Christian people may not of right say unto God this that followeth: *Incerta et occulta sapientiæ tuæ manifestasti mihi?* " Good Lord, Thou hast shewed unto me the mysteries of Thine infinite wisdom, which before were hid and unknown to us?" But why hath God shewed us these secrets? What doth it profit, the secret mysteries of Him to be shewed and made open to us? What comfort shall we take by it? Truly great comfort if we unfeignedly repent our old sinful life: else we know them to our great hurt. For, as St. Peter saith *Melius est non cognoscere viam justitiæ, quam post agnitionem retrorsum converti.* " It is better not to know the way of rightwiseness than after the knowledge of it to use and do the contrary." But if we turn to God and follow His commandments, forsaking our wretched life, having faith and trust in His sacraments, we shall without doubt obtain forgiveness and mercy by the virtue of them.

Peradventure some man shall say,"we see what is done in every sacrament. In the sacrament of Baptism the child is washed in the water, and a few words be spoken of the priest. In the Confirmation, the forehead of the child is anointed with holy cream[1] in manner of a cross, with a few words spoken of[2] the priest. In the Sacrament of Penance after the Confession is heard and the satisfaction enjoined, the priest saith also a few words. What belongeth these to the health of the soul? For the words, anon as they be spoken, be gone into the air and nothing of them remaineth. The water also and the oil pierceth not from the body unto the soul." Perchance some man will think this in himself. And it is of a truth the water and the oil to have no strength of their own nature whereby they may enter unto the soul, or to work in it good or evil. Nevertheless, there is a privy and hid virtue given unto them by the merits of the Passion of Jesus Christ and of His Precious Blood, which on the Cross was shed for wretched sinners. This most holy and dear Blood of Jesus Christ shed for our redemption, bought and gave so great and plenteous virtue to the sacraments, that as often as any creature shall use and receive any of them, so often it is to be believed they are sprinkled with the drops of the same most holy

[1] chrism.   [2] by.

Blood, whose virtue pierceth unto the soul, and maketh it clean from all sin. But whereby know we this? Truly for He hath shewed and made open the hid and uncertain things to us of His infinite wisdom. It was a custom in the Old Law amongst the Jews to do away their sins by this manner. If any of them by touching of a dead body or by any other manner thing were culpable and made foul, anon he was made clean of that default with hyssop dipped in the blood of certain beasts and sprinkled upon him. Which manner and custom was given to the Jews by Moses, and ordained by the wisdom of God. Nevertheless at that time it was unknown what this matter meant and signified. It was uncertain, it was hid, what the wisdom of God would to be understood by this aspersion or sprinkling of blood. And after that our Blessed Lord Jesus Christ had shed His Precious Blood, and, as saith St. Peter, washed us from sin with His Blood, it was known to every man what by the hyssop and by the aspersion of blood was signified. Hyssop is an herb of the ground that of its nature is hot, and hath a sweet smell, signifying Christ which meeked Himself to suffer death on the Cross. And, as St. Paul saith, He offered Himself of very great and fervent charity unto His Father Almighty God as a sacrifice of sweet odour. No man may doubt of this, that by the aspersion of blood of beasts before the Incarnation was signified and represented the effusion of the Blood of Christ for our redemption. Which Blood of our Saviour without doubt is of much more strength incomparably to do away sins than was the blood of beasts. And as often as the holy sacraments be iterated and used according to the commandment of Christ's Church, so often is the blessed Blood of our Lord sprinkled abroad to cleanse and put away sin. Therefore let us all say with the holy prophet this verse that followeth: *Asperges me, Domine, hyssopo et mundabor:* as we might say, " Lord, our faith is so clear and undoubtful by the merit of the Passion of Thy Son our Lord Jesus Christ, Which by the effusion of His holy Blood hath given so great efficacy and strength to the holy sacraments of His Church, that when we receive any of them we shall be sprinkled and made clean by the virtue of His Precious Blood like as with hyssop. Which aspersion anon followeth the water of grace that is infused in our souls, whereby we be made more white than snow." Therefore the prophet addeth to the same verse: *Lavabis me et super nivem dealbabor:* " Lord, Thou shalt wash me and I shall be made more white than snow." No creature may express how joyful the sinner is when he knoweth and understandeth himself to be delivered from the great burden and heaviness of sin, when he seeth and perceiveth that he is delivered utterly and brought out of the danger of so many and great perils that he was in whilst he continued in sin, when also he perceiveth the clearness of his soul and remembereth the tranquillity and peace of his conscience. *Audit tunc quid loquatur intra se Dominus, quoniam loquetur pacem in servos suos et in eos qui convertuntur ad cor:* " Then he perceiveth well in his heart what our Lord will shew in him by inspiration." What shall He shew? Everlasting peace to come upon His servants, upon them that be sorrowful and do penance for their sins. Which peace is so joyful and comfortable and causeth so great joy and gladness that the prophet remembering it saith: *Auditui meo dabis gaudium et lætitiam:* " Lord, Thou shalt give to mine hearing inwardly joy and gladness." If the peace of this time be so greatly to be desired to the inward hearing of our soul, what joy, trow we, shall be at that time when the peace everlasting shall be offered to us, when the King of Eternal Peace shall say unto all true penitent persons: *Venite, benedicti Patris mei, percipite regnum quod vobis paratum est a constitutione mundi:* " Come to Me, ye blessed children of My Father, take the everlasting kingdom that was prepared and made ready for you before the beginning of the world." Shall we not joy then inwardly in our souls, shall we not joy then outwardly in our bodies, shall we not then joy both body and soul without adversity, never to cease? Shall not this fearful Judge saying these comfortable words give unto our hearing inward joy of the soul for the salvation of it? Shall He not give fervent joy when we have obtained our asking and our desire? Shall He not give everlasting joy without any adversity? Truly He shall give inward joy for the sorrow of our contrition, joy also for weeping in our confession, and lastly everlasting joy for the grief of our satisfaction. *Et tunc exultabunt ossa humiliata:* that is to say, the superior strengths of the soul, which be called Will, Reason, and Memory, that before were overthrown by the grievance of sin, shall then joy for ever without any adversity. Our will shall joy in the fruition of God; our reason, in the clear sight of the Godhead. And lastly our memory shall joy in a sure remembrance ever to continue, and never lack that excellent joy and pleasure. Then our will, our reason, and our memory, before oppressed and brought under by sin, shall joy without end.

That we promised in our beginning is now performed and shewed in this first part of the Psalm. First what thing we that be penitent should ask; second, what reasons we may make and bring for ourself for the grant of our petition; and last, that we may trust without doubt to obtain our asking. Which our Lord grant us. Amen.

AVERTE FACIEM TUAM A PECCATIS MEIS ET OMNES INIQUITATES MEAS DELE

PSALM l (Part II)

FOR as much as we have so greatly praised the mercy of God in the end of the first part of this Psalm, whereby we have given to all sinners great confidence to obtain forgiveness, it is now to be thought profitable or ever[1] we speak of this second part, somewhat to shew of the fear of Almighty God. Many great causes there be to trust of forgiveness if we consider the great mercy of God, so often shewed upon penitent sinners. Also we have many great causes to fear Almighty God, if we remember how many and great our sins be, wherewith we

---

[1] ere.

H

daily offend His goodness. Therefore sith we have so good and many just causes both of hope and dread, (as me seemeth) he taketh the most sure way that maketh the one meet with the other: that is to say, hope with dread and dread with hope. That person which so doth, shall neither trust in God without His fear, nor dread Him without hope; for by inclining more to the one than to the other we shall soon err; either, by overmuch hope, to be exalted into very presumption; or, by overmuch fear, to be cast down into the most ungracious danger of despair. But he that mixeth the one with the other in even portions shall neither be lifted up by presumption nor cast down by despair. Nothing is more profitable to the sinner than to have a just moderation of them both. And nothing is more perilous than leaning more to the one than to the other. For the which thing St. Gregory compareth hope and dread unto two millstones wherewith meal is made. So it is, one millstone without a fellow made meet can do no good; but if the one be made fit with the other, that is to say the over stone turned downward and the nether contrariwise against it up-ward, with a due proportion of both, then shall the wheat put in the midst between them be shortly broken into many small pieces and in conclusion to meal. Likewise it is with sinners when hope is mixed with dread and dread with hope, so that by overmuch hope of forgive-ness the mind be not lifted up into presumption, and by overmuch fear it be not put down into despair. Then if the multitude of sins be never so great, they shall shortly between these two be broken into many small parts and in conclusion utterly done away. But why say we thus? Truly to the intent,[1] although the certainty of forgiveness be never so great, yet a remembrance be ever had of the fear of Almighty God, never to put it out of mind. As St. Peter did: knowing that his sin was forgiven, notwithstanding, he wept daily for his unkind-ness against his Lord and Master, ever after remember-ing how unkindly he denied Him. Also blessed Mary Magdalene, which heard Christ forgive her sins for the

[1] *supply* that.

great love she had unto Him, for all that took upon her great penance, ever having in mind the filthiness of her sin committed before. She busied herself by continually weeping to put it away utterly from the sight of Almighty God. Our prophet doth in like manner, shewing example to all sinners of doing the same, and that after he had full hope and trust to be forgiven of God. Know it for a surety by those things which he understood in the hid and uncertain[1] privities of the wisdom of our Lord God. Albeit, anon he returned to the remembrance of his sins, saying *Averte faciem tuam a peccatis meis:* " Blessed Lord, turn away Thy face from my sins."

In our beginning we shall divide the residue of this Psalm into three parts. In the first our prophet maketh a new petition; in the second he sheweth the intent of his petition, which is that he may please God; in the third he teacheth that his Desire is the chief thing whereby every man may please God and make recompense for sin.

I. The thing asked is the Spirit of God, the Holy Ghost, which is never but in clean hearts; as Sapiens[2] saith, *Non enim habitabit in corpore subdito peccatis:* " The Holy Ghost shall not dwell or abide in a body subject to sin." Almighty God hateth nothing so much as sin, and punisheth nothing so grievously; it is abominable in His sight. First in Heaven, where sin was in the angels, anon as many as were infected with it Almighty God put down and cast out of that Heavenly palace and would not spare those noble and goodly creatures. After, when that same pestiferous infection of sin infected our first fathers in Paradise, He would not spare, but anon put them out of that pleasant place into this vale of wretchedness. Albeit, after many generations, Almighty God chose the people of Israel which came of them, notwithstanding, when some began for to be contaminated or defiled with the infection of sin, (as is shewed of Dathan and Abiron with many others) the earth opened by the power of Almighty God and swallowed them in quick. Thus Almighty God expulsed sin, first out of Heaven,

---

[1] mysterious.   [2] The writer of Book of Wisdom.

after from Paradise, and out of the earth; in so much, when this infection was spread abroad upon all the earth, in the time of the patriarch Noe He drowned almost all mankind. And lastly when sin could not be utterly expulsed by all these punishments, He sent down into this world His only-begotten Son to suffer death and shed His Precious Blood for the redemption of all wretched sinners.

Let us therefore consider how abominable sin is in the sight of Almighty God, when first He put out of Heaven His first creatures the angels; our first fathers. out of Paradise; His special chosen people, from the earth; drowned almost all mankind; and lastly He suffered His only Son for to die upon a cross for the redemption of all wretched sinners. All these He did to the intent sin should only remain in the deep pit of Hell.

Peradventure our prophet, remembering this abomination of sin, feared in himself, and for that cause saith: *Averte faciem tuam a peccatis meis:* " Good Lord, look not upon my sins." Forasmuch as Almighty God cannot well turn away His face from our sins (as long as they be fixed in our souls) but also He must turn away His face from us. As, by this example, who may perceive and see a wall painted with many divers images, but first He must look upon those same pictures? For they be as a veil or covering to the wall, wherefore needs the sight must first be applied unto them. In like manner therefore since our sins in respect of the soul be to it as a picture or covering is to a wall, Almighty God must needs first look upon our sins or ever He look upon our souls. Alas what shall we sinful wretches do? Certainly this only remedy is necessary: whoso will look upon a bare wall, must first do away the painting or covering; and that done all shall be clean and pure to behold. So if our souls should be seen and not our sins, first our sins must be clean done away; for all the while they be infected with the least spot of sin, so long they may not be seen without the sin be seen also. Our prophet therefore prayeth to Almighty God that all his sins may be utterly done away, to the intent that he may clearly look upon his soul without any let. *Et omnes iniquitates meas dele:* " Good Lord, do away all my sins." But it is not enough all sins to be done away, without the fountain whereof they spring out be clean and purified. For if it be so that the stinking filthy water continually flow out of a pond or pit into a goodly and delectable garden, if remedy be not found to stop the same, it shall make foul and corrupt that garden within a while, be it never so fair. So in like wise shall it be with us if the heart be not first made clean. For our Saviour saith *De corde exeunt cogitationes malæ, homicidia, adulteria, fornicationes, furta, falsa testimonia, blasphemiæ:* "From the heart cometh out evil thoughts, manslaughter, adultery, fornication, theft, false witness, and blasphemy." Take heed what pestiferous corruption cometh from the heart, whereby all the whole body and soul is defiled; for, as it followeth in the same text, *Hæc sunt quæ coinquinant hominem:* " These be the corruptions which make foul both body and soul." Therefore all sins may not be clean done away but if[1] the heart, whereof continually they come, be first made clean. For this cause our prophet asketh of Almighty God, saying *Cor mundum crea in me Deus:* " Lord, make within me a clean heart." Many craftsmen had liefer take upon them to make a thing all new than to botch or mend an old foreworn thing, as we see by experience. Better it were for the artificer to make a clock all new than to mend, or bring again into the right course, a clock which long hath continued out of its right order. But it is much more diffuse[2] to bring the heart of man that is broken and brought out of good order by continual custom of sin into the right way again than it is to bring a clock into its true course. A thing customably used is hard to be left. And, as St. Augustine saith, it is more hard work to bring the heart of a man long customed in sin into the way of virtue, than it is to make again heaven and earth. Our prophet for this cause beseecheth Almighty God, to Whom is nothing impossible, that He vouchsafe for to create within him a new heart, saying *Cor mundum crea in me,*

---

[1] unless.   [2] complicated.

Deus: " Good Lord, make Thou of nought a clean heart within me." Moreover it is necessary that a new work be set in a right course. For what profiteth a clock, be it never so well and craftily made, if it stand still or go not as it should in a due and just course? Truly nothing. So when the heart is once made new, first it must be set in a due and right course. Wherefore the prophet addeth *Et spiritum rectum innova in visceribus meis:* " Blessed Lord, grant me the Holy Ghost to guide and set me in a right way that I err not."

The prophet in this Psalm nameth thrice the Holy Spirit, by and by.[1] What he meaneth is uncertain, and I of myself dare not take upon me to discuss the cause of his so doing. But forasmuch as it is lawful for every clerk in any such doubts to shew their minds, not contrarying other places of Scripture, I shall in few words declare (as me seemeth) what he meaneth. I doubt not in this. The Holy Ghost in Scripture is signified by these three names rehearsed in this Psalm. St. Paul, remembering the divers gifts or deeds of the Holy Ghost, saith: *Hæc omnia operatur unus atque idem Spiritus:* " One Spirit without change doth all." I say the prophet rehearsing divers names of the Holy Ghost saith *Spiritum sapientiæ et intellectus spiritum consilii et fortitudinis, spiritum scientiæ et pietatis ac spiritum timoris Domini:* " The Spirit of wisdom and understanding, the Spirit of counsel and strength, the Spirit of cunning and piety, and the Spirit of the fear of God ": he meaneth not so many divers spirits, but One, called by so many names for the diversity of His acts. But (for so much as shall be convenient for our purpose at this season) we read in the holy Gospels the shewing of the Holy Ghost thrice in three divers similitudes. Once the Holy Ghost came down in the likeness of a dove when Christ was baptized ; as it appeareth in the Gospel of Luke: *Et descendit Spiritus corporali specie sicut columba in eum.* Also after Christ's Resurrection, was given in the likeness of a breath to the disciples of Jesus, as in the Gospel of John: *Et insufflavit in eos dicens: Accipite*

[1] successively.

Spiritum Sanctum: quorum remiseritis peccata, remittuntur eis.' Thirdly, when after Christ's Ascension the Holy Ghost appeared to the Apostles, gathered all together, in the likeness of fire: as is shewed in the Gospel of Luke *Apparuerunt illis dispertitæ linguæ tanquam ignis seditque supra singulos eorum Spiritus Sanctus.* Which three divers appearings signify three divers gifts of the Holy Ghost given to three divers states or kinds of people; that is to say, first to them which be infants at their Baptism; second, to penitents; and third, to them that be perfect.

First at our Baptism we be directed and set in a new life, the life of innocency, which is signified by the dove appearing over Christ at His Baptism. St. Paul exhorteth all such, saying *Novitate vitæ ambulent:* " That they walk in a new life." And Christ saith *Ut sint simplices sicut columbæ:* " Meekly, in manner as doves." The prophet, remembering this operation of the Holy Ghost, saith *Et spiritum rectum innova in visceribus meis:* " Blessed Lord, grant me the Holy Ghost to set me in a new life of innocency."

The other operation is according for them that be penitent; which, as we said, was given to the Apostles under the likeness of a breath. We see by experience, a man's breathing when it touches anything that is cold, as iron or glass, anon it is resolved into weeping drops of water. Which thing may be oftentimes perceived in a penitent sinner. Sins make the heat of charity to wax cold, as our Saviour saith *Ubi abundabit iniquitas, refrigescet charitas:* " Where sin is abundant, charity waxeth cold." When the sinner is pricked in his conscience by the Holy Ghost, remembering the abomination of his sins, anon (if he be very penitent) tears shall trickle down from his eyes. Which is a great token the Holy Ghost is present with that sinner: as Scripture saith, *Flabit spiritus ejus et fluent aquæ.* On this wise Christ our Saviour looked upon Peter, after he had denied Him, with a gracious countenance or breath of His Holy Spirit; and forthwith he fell on a-weeping: as in the Gospel of John, *Conversus Dominus respexit Petrum, et egressus*

/oras flevit amare: " Our Saviour turned back and looked upon Peter; and, incontinent, Peter went out and wept bitterly." Sin defileth the soul and turneth the face of God away from it. But this gift of the Holy Ghost, penance with weeping tears, washeth the soul, maketh it holy and causeth Almighty God to look again upon it with His merciful countenance. Therefore our prophet saith *Ne projicias me a facie tua et spiritum sanctum tuum ne auferas a me:* " Blessed Lord, cast me not out of Thy sight, take not Thy holy Spirit from me, give me grace to know my sins, to confess them and to do penance with weeping tears,"—teaching all sinners busily to pray Almighty God, if at any season by our own negligence we offend His goodness, notwithstanding, He vouchsafe not to cast us away from His sight but again look on us, and give us grace to weep for our offences: whereby our souls may be made holy. And if it shall please Him thus to look upon us, our sins shall be utterly done away; and, by our weeping, the punishment for the same. O most meek Jesus, what caused Thee to look so mercifully upon Peter? He was baptized before, had the spirit of continuance in virtue; Thou gavest him example always to live rightwisely, he alway beheld Thine holy conversation, heard Thine holy preachings, saw Thy great miracles, He was present at Thy Transfiguration, heard the voice of the Father saying " Thou art My Son." And for all this he denied Thee, whereas before Thou gave him warning, and shewed he should so do. O Blessed Lord, where might have been shewed more unkindness? Good Jesus, we beseech Thee look upon us wretched sinners in like manner, which never yet denied Thee, neither had so great knowledge and helps to live well as he had. If the sin of Peter moved Thee to mercy and forgiveness, Blessed Lord, we be sinners also; Thou art now as meek and merciful as ever Thou wert before, and we be turned to Thee asking forgiveness. Since Thou, undesired, looked so mercifully and forgave Peter, we beseech Thee deny not to forgive us which ask forgiveness incessantly. *Ne projicias nos a facie tua et Spiritum Sanctum tuum ne auferas a nobis:* " Blessed

Lord, put us not out of Thy sight, take not Thy Holy Spirit away from us, grant that we may weep for our sins."

The third operation of the Holy Ghost is much more strong than any of the others: whereby they which be perfect be made steadfast in all virtue without any wavering. It was given to the Apostles of Christ in the likeness of fire. 'And or ever[1] this gift of the Holy Ghost was given unto them they were not steadfast in the faith, they were fearful and wavering in their minds; which was well perceived by[1] Peter, that offered himself to die for His Master's sake, and notwithstanding, anon after, denied Him unto a woman. But as soon as they were endued with this gift of the Holy Ghost, all worldly vanities were utterly despised among them, they feared no man. *Gaudentes ibant a conspectu consilii quoniam digni habiti sunt pro nomine Jesu contumeliam pati:* "For they were joyful coming from their judgments, because they should suffer shame and death for the Name of Jesus." Our prophet therefore in this place nameth the Holy Ghost the third time, saying *Et spiritu principali confirma me:* "Lord, make me steadfast in faith and charity by the grace of the Holy Ghost, that never after I fall again to sin." But we have left out the first part of this verse. So it is: after our Saviour Jesus Christ (Which our prophet calleth oftentimes " *Salutare* ") ascended into Heaven, and, according as He promised, should send down the Holy Ghost (as we said) in the similitude of fire, they were very sad and sorry for their Master's departing, Jesus; but, anon as they had received that marvellous comfort of the Holy Ghost, great gladness came into them, unable to be told, so that all the people standing by thought them to be drunken of sweet wine. Therefore our prophet called that comfort sent down from our Lord Jesus Christ *lætitiam Salutaris:* " a gladness of our 'Saviour." For when a messenger bringeth a gladful message from anybody, it may be called a comfort both of him that sendeth the message and of him that bringeth it. So this gladness, sent from

[1] in the instance of.

the Father of Heaven by His Son Jesus Christ, is called a gladness or comfort of them both. Therefore David saith unto Almighty God the Father *Redde mihi lœtitiam Salutaris tui et spiritu principali confirma me:* " Lord, give again to me the gladness of Thy Son Jesus Christ our Saviour, which I lost by my sinful life, and strengthen me with the Holy Ghost that I never fall again to sin."

Hitherto we have spoken of the petition wherein is asked the Holy Ghost by three divers names; first our prophet calleth Him *Spiritum rectum,* after that *Spiritum sanctum,* and third *Spiritum principalem.* The cause why, we have declared after our mind. And because no man may receive the Holy Ghost but with a clean heart, no man can be clean in heart but if his sins be utterly done away, and sins cannot be clean done away if Almighty God turn not away His face from them, therefore our prophet asked meekly these three, as three means whereby he might obtain his finable[1] intent, which is the gift of the Holy Ghost for his confirmation and perseverance in good life.

II. In this second part our prophet sheweth the cause why he desired the Holy Ghost for his petition: which was to the intent he might profit his neighbour. It is very good and acceptable to God when one person, seeing another err and do evil, will meekly with good and sweet words give him warning to leave his wickedness, and bring him again into the right way whereby he may come to God. St. James saith, he that so doth deserveth a great reward: which is the promise of salvation and doing away of his own sins. These be his words: *Qui converti fecerit peccatorem ab errore viœ suœ, salvabit animam ejus a morte et operit multitudinem peccatorum:* " Whosoever caused a sinner to leave his sinful life shall both save his own soul from damnation and his sin to be done away." Which words are not only to be understood of them that have authority to rebuke sin, but also of all Christian people; for every person in manner[2] hath

---

[1] final.   [2] in some sort.

charge of others. Thus, when one seeth another do evil, he ought to give him warning charitably of his so doing; and peradventure in such manner we should do more good and win more souls to God than by open rebuking. And truly our doing is but small if we may not, after the knowledge of our own errors done before, give others warning to amend their life when they do amiss. Notwithstanding, an order must be kept in this matter: it is not lawful for every man to teach at his pleasure. For he that shall give instruction to others must first know both the way of well doing and evil, else he shall soon bring his brother out of the right way. Our Saviour saith *Si cæcus cæco ducatum præstet, ambo in foveam cadunt:* "If one blind lead another, both fall into the ditch." To take the office of a doctor or teacher of God's laws is no small charge, it is a great jeopardy; wherein I myself, remembering the same, am often afraid; for many times I think on St. Paul's saying: *Væ mihi si non evangelizavero:* "If I teach not the laws of God unto the people, I shall be damned." I fear me, if we hide that gift of God, if we give not a good account of that talent, lest it shall be said to us at the dreadful Day of Judgment, as it is written in the Gospel, *Quare non dedisti pecuniam meam ad mensam?* "Why gave thou not to me a true and just account of my money?" That is to say, of the learning which I gave unto thee, wherewith thou shouldst have taught the people My laws. Also if we teach and by it profit the hearers, yet is great peril lest when any praise is given to us for our learning we be not stricken with pride and vainglory when we know ourself praised. The miserable corruption of our nature is so caduke[1] that, when we do anything never so little praiseworthy, it is a marvel if we offend not in vainglory. But, of a truth, if a due order be had in our teaching of others, as we said before, every man according to his learning and ability: that is to say, if first we study for the amendment of our own life, purge our own souls, be about as much as we may to learn the wisdom of our Lord, and by our busy prayer ask of God

[1] prone to fall.

the cleansing of our hearts, with the grace of the Holy Ghost, whereby we may order our own steps in the way of God, not for the vain praise of the world but only to bring them which err into the right ways, that they by our living and doctrine be turned to that blessed Lord. Which doing shall be to the honour of God and profit to our neighbours. To this purpose it followeth: *Docebo iniquos vias tuas, et impii ad te convertentur:* as he might say, " Blessed Lord, if Thou look not upon my sins but do away my wickedness, create in me a new heart and endue me with the gift of the Holy Ghost, I shall teach them that err, bring them into Thy ways, and they shall be turned to worship Thee." Truly the prophet after his great offence kept this said order. St. Paul also after his great persecution of Christ's Church, made clean, and inspired with the Holy Ghost, taught openly to all people the right way to come unto Heaven, made open to all wicked creatures the ways of Almighty God. Christ our Saviour giveth us all warning so to do, saying *Si peccaverit in te frater tuus corripe eum:* " If thy neighbour or brother offend thee, correct him charitably." Therefore let every one of us ask of Almighty God a clean heart and the Holy Ghost, to the intent we may teach wicked people the ways of salvation, that they may the sooner turn to Him by our doctrine.

But why make we no mention of the other two gifts or receivings of the Holy Ghost? Truly lest we should break the due order of them rehearsed. For the prophet asketh three divers gifts of the Holy Ghost, and rehearseth the causes why, one after another. We have spoken of the first named *spiritus rectus,* which, as we said, is given to every person in the time of their Baptism. Now shall we shew of the other two, and both by themselves.

The second gift of the Holy Ghost, called the spirit of penance, which maketh holy all true penitents, was set in the second place: the reason why followeth now in this second part. The abominable corruption of sin in many places of Scripture is compared to corrupt blood. It is said unto all sinners: *Manus vestræ plenæ sunt*

sanguine: " Your hands be replete with corrupt blood ":
to say,[1] our works be sinful. Peradventure the most corruption of blood is caused by carnal concupiscence.
Therefore St. Paul saith *Caro et sanguis regnum Dei non
possidebunt:* " Flesh and blood shall not have the Kingdom of Heaven in possession ": as much to say, they that
be corrupt by bodily or fleshly desire shall never come to
Heaven without amendment. Like as a language spoken
hath its beginning of the tongue and is commonly called
the tongue (as we say our " mother tongue," and commonly it is said he speaketh in many " tongues " which
can speak many languages) ; so likewise sin, which is
chiefly caused of blood, is called " blood," and many
sins many " bloods." For this cause in the Old Law
blood of beasts was shed for cleansing of sins, whereby
Almighty God might be rather appeased against the filthiness of sin.   St. Paul saith *Omnia in sanguine munda-
bantur et sine sanguine non fit remissio:* " All sins were
made clean by effusion of blood, and without it was no
remission." But doubtless the effusion of that blood, of
the own strength and virtue, might never purge sin ; the
bloody corruption could not be expulsed from our souls
by it, according as St. Paul saith, *Impossibile est sanguine hircorum et taurorum auferri peccata:* " It is impossible sins to be done away by the effusion of goats'
blood or bulls'."   Notwithstanding, that shedding of
blood prefigured the effusion of the most precious Blood
of Christ Jesus upon a cross plenteously for all sinners :
whereby satisfaction was made to God the Father for the
sins of all people, which receive the virtue of this precious Blood by the sacraments of Christ's Church, and
by it made rightwise. Percase[2] a sinful wretch cometh
to a priest, sheweth all his sins, sheddeth out from his
breast corrupt blood of sin, in manner as the throat of a
beast were cut or a filthy wound lanced with a lance ;
afterwards the Sacrament of Penance is ministered to
him by his ghostly father, wherewith by the virtue of
Christ's precious Blood he is made clean from sin, and
then verily justified. He came to his ghostly father as

[1] that is to say.   [2] suppose.

a sinful person, but by the virtue of this Sacrament of Penance he goeth away from him rightwise, not by his own rightwiseness, but by the rightwiseness of Christ Jesus, Who rightwisely redeemed us with His precious Blood, as St. John saith in the Apocalypse, and St. Paul sheweth, *Factus est nobis justitia.* Therefore we sinners have great cause to magnify and praise the rightwiseness of Jesus Christ, whereby He maketh us of unrightwise to be rightwise, and by the virtue of His precious Blood delivered from the abomination of sin. For the which cause the prophet asked before the spirit of penance, that the bloody spots of sin might be done away by it, to the intent he might shew everlastingly the rightwiseness of God, saying *Libera me de sanguinibus, Deus, Deus salutis meæ, et exultabit lingua mea justitiam tuam:* " Blessed Lord, deliver me from the corruption of sin and my tongue shall joy eternally Thy rightwiseness."

The third spirit or gift of the Holy Ghost that he asked was the spirit of confirmation or making steadfast in virtue, which was given to the Apostles at the day of Pentecost in the likeness of fiery tongues. After the receiving of it they were so constant and steadfast in the love of God that except Him they feared no man. They testified over all[1] the Name of Jesus without dread, they kept together the unsteadfast people by their holy words, shewing over all[1] the Name of Jesus Christ to the laud and praise of Almighty God. A marvellous thing that they being so rude, neither taught by Plato nor Aristotle or any other philosopher, but getting their living by fishing, should so marvellously dispute and show the magnificence of Christ before so wise, so great, and prudent men of this world, insomuch they plainly convinced and entreated them at their pleasure. But, blessed Lord, Thy wisdom gave them that grace, Thou gavest them fiery tongues, Thou opened their lips, Which of Thy goodness made infants to speak in laud of Thy magnificence. Thy prophet Isaie at such times as he durst not take upon him to speak Thy holy words, said *Vir pollutus labiis ego sum et in medio populi polluta labia habentis ego habito:*

---

[1] everywhere.

" Blessed Lord, my lips be polluted and I am abiding amongst the people which in like manner be unclean." One of Thy angels came unto him, touched his mouth, made clean his lips, and forthwith he was made very bold and shewed himself ready to do Thy commandment in expressing unto the people Thy law of truth. Likewise our prophet prayeth that his lips may be made clean and himself steadfast and constant in virtue by the grace of the Holy Ghost, to the intent he might worthily shew Thy lauds. He saith *Domine, labia mea aperies et os meum annuntiabit laudem tuam:* " Good Lord, open my lips, make them clean, and my mouth shall shew over all Thy praise or laud." Let us follow this prophet David, beseeching Almighty God that first He make us able and worthy to receive the Holy Ghost, grant us His grace to live rightfully, also to admonish (according as we be called in degree) our neighbours unto penance, whereby ourself may be made holy and delivered clean from all sin, to praise and exalt the rightwiseness of God; and lastly that we may have the third gift of the Holy Ghost, which is to be made steadfast and constant with clean lips to shew over all the lauds of Almighty God.

In this third part our prophet sheweth, nothing[1] so acceptable to God which he may give to Him in recompense of his sins, as is this that he hath spoken of now before. The manner of Jews was (in the Old Law) when any of them had broken the commandment of God, for making amends, to hallow a certain part of a beast or else the whole, after[2] as the greatness of the sin required. Moses taught the unlearned people by such bodily sacrifices: which was to them as a shadow or figure of the true Sacrifice to come, that was first signified by them. The slaying of those brute beasts, after Moses' intent, figured the death of our Saviour Christ Jesus; and ever he busied himself to cause the people believe it by those tokens. For as the unreasonable[3] beast was slain for cleansing of sins, and the blood of it shed upon the altar, so Christ Jesus, the Lamb undefiled, most innocent beast, was put to death upon a cross and all His Blood shed for the re-

---

[1] that nothing is.   [2] according.   [3] irrational.

mission of sinners. The people of Israel sinned and were worthy to die for it; those brute beasts did none evil and yet were put to death for the amendment of their sins. Likewise our Saviour Christ: although He was most innocent, most pure, and never offended in any condition, notwithstanding, he suffered death most patiently for our offences. The slaying of beasts that was used in the Old Law for their sacrifice did not please God very well of themself, as He shewed in another place, in manner reproving them, saying *Numquid manducabo carnes taurorum aut sanguinem hircorum potabo?* " Shall I eat the flesh of bulls or drink the blood of goats?" as who saith, " It is not my pleasure so to do." If Almighty God might be appeased or caused to show mercy by no other remedy but by the oblation of brute beasts, poor men were then in miserable condition that wanted power to make such oblation, if they might not be otherwise forgiven, but to die in their sins. But Almighty God hath ordained more even laws, which be common both to poor and rich; He desireth none other sacrifice but such as the poor may do as soon as the rich, and peradventure more soon, for Almighty God taketh more heed to the good intent of the mind than to the greatness or value of the gift. Which thing is shewed in the Gospel of Mark, where is expressed that when Jesus perceived and beheld the rich folks offer many great gifts into the treasure-house, among all He espied a poor widow which gave only two mites, and said that poor woman offered most of all, not regarding the greatness of the gift, but only, (as we said) the good mind and intent of the doer. Whereby we may well perceive that since the acceptable sacrifice to God dependeth not by[1] the value of the gift but by[1] the good mind and intent of the doer, also that He is not well pleased with such manner sacrifice of the Old Law although it were done by a thousand beasts, therefore our prophet saith *Quoniam si voluisses sacrificium dedissem; utique holocaustis non delectaberis.* *Sacrificium* was called a part of the beast offered, and *holocaustum* the whole oblation of it; since the whole was

[1] on.

not delectable to God in sacrifice, the part was much less acceptable. Our prophet here remembereth another manner sacrifice which is most acceptable to God, and it is named the very penance of man's soul. A question may be asked what offence committed the unreasonable beast that his blood should be shed? Truly nothing: therefore no just cause or reason can be shewed why they should die. But the sinful creature which so grievously hath displeased God his Maker, following his own sensual and unlawful volupty against the will of our Lord God, of very right ought to suffer as much displeasure and pain as he had pleasure before in the sensual and unrightwise appetite of his body. Then shall he make a due and just recompense for his sins. That penitent spirit is the sacrifice whereby Almighty God is chiefly appeased and moved to shew mercy. It followeth: *Sacrificium Deo spiritus contribulatus:* " The sorrowful and penitent soul is chief sacrifice to God for purging of sins." Our Saviour Christ Jesus shewed in the Gospel of Luke two men entered into the Temple to pray, one of them a Pharisee, the other a Publican. Among the Jews Pharisees shewed outward in their living a more holy life and conversation than other did, they exercised holy works in the sight of the people; the Publicans contrariwise gave heed and occupied themselves in worldly and covetous business with all manner vices. As they were praying in the Temple, first the Pharisee lauded God of his holy conversation, praised himself, remembering his merits in manner[1] to the dispraise of all other, thought none able to be compared to him, said, " I am far unlike to other (in my living) that commit theft and adultery as doth this Publican. I live chaste, I fast twice in the week and abstain from all other vices, I give tithes of all my goods." Thus proudly the Pharisee boasted and praised himself in his virtue. The Publican contrariwise, calling to mind the multitude of his sins and meekly remembering the holiness of the Temple that he was in, both for fear and reverence stood afar, ashamed in himself for the filthiness of his sins, durst not lift up his eyes to Heaven, but with a great in-

[1] in some sort.

I

ward sorrow knocked upon his breast, acknowledged himself a grievous sinner, humbly asking the mercy of God, and said *Deus propitius esto mihi peccatori:* " Blessed Lord, be merciful to me a sinner ": the penance and contrition of his heart was so great. Whereby he gave so acceptable sacrifice to Almighty God that by it he was clean forgiven and the Pharisee reject.   Take heed how acceptable sacrifice to Almighty God is a sorrowful and contrite heart for sin.   Was not Achab, sometime King of Israel, reconciled and forgiven by such manner sacrifice after his great and innumerable offences?   It is written that he lived most wickedly, breaking the commandment of God more than all kings of Israel before him ; he did sacrifice unto the false God Baal and favoured the priests of his law, chased away and despised the prophets of God ; notwithstanding, our merciful Lord of His goodness would chastise him by shewing many wonders and strange tokens.   First He caused that no rain fell on the earth by the space of three years and three months, to the intent Achab the King should know Almighty God was discontented with him.   Also another time in the sight of all the people He gave so great virtue to His prophet Elias that, at his desire and calling, fire came down from heaven which consumed and utterly took away their present sacrifice.   Furthermore after the long continuance without rain, when Achab mistrusted, by the petition of the said Elias water came down from heaven plenteously.   What creature would not amend himself by these wonderful tokens?   But Achab was never the better, continued still in his malice : notwithstanding, our Lord God of His gentleness proved him again by other means.   When Benadab king of Assyria came to subdue Achab with a great host of people, Almighty God would not suffer him to be betrayed of his adversary, but promised he should have the victory. Another time, the year after, when the same Benadab had recovered his strength, he came upon him afresh in battle.   Whereof Almighty God gave him monition by His prophet and promised he should have the victory. Furthermore, when he would not amend himself but rather was worse and worse, insomuch he caused the rightwise man Naboth to be slain and by guile got his vineyard, then Almighty God threatened him, saying *Se demessurum omnem posteritatem ipsius et interjecturum de Achab mingentem ad parietem:* " He should put down all his posterity and slay all that came of him and not leave scant a dog." Achab, hearing this, was anon compunct and sorrowed his misliving; he cut and rent his clothes, went in hair next his body, fasted, lay nightly in sackcloth, and held down his head. Our blessed Lord seeing his great penance and meekness was moved with pity, said unto his prophet Elias *Nonne vidisti humiliatum Achab coram me? Et quia humiliatus est mei causa, non inducam malum in diebus ejus:* " Seest thou not the meekness of Achab, perceivest thou not how he hath meeked himself before Me? And because of his so doing for My cause, I will not shew vengeance in his days." O merciful Lord, why did Thou so, why did Thou refrain from ire, why shewed Thou not vengeance upon that most ungentle creature? Truly for in him was a sorrowful and a contrite soul, which is the chief sacrifice, whereby Thou art caused to shew mercy. *Sacrificium Deo spiritus contribulatus, cor contritum et humiliatum, Deus, non despicies:* " The sorrowful and penitent soul is chief sacrifice to God, and, Blessed Lord, Thou shalt not despise a contrite heart." Whosoever ordereth himself on this manner that by his inward sorrow he may have a contrite heart, he is able and meet unto the high building in the Heavenly City whose walls be not yet finished. A great number of stones is wanting wherewith they should be performed and accomplished, for the ruin of angels which fell down from that City must be repaired and renewed by taking up of men and women, like as by quick stones. As we see in manner when stones be assumpt[1] for the re-edifying of cities or towers with other. But it is according that into such a noble building no stone be taken up, but if[2] that it be prepared as it should be and made meet before. For in that Heavenly Palace may no stone be polished, shapen

---

[1] taken up.   [2] unless.

or made square. It must be made fit and perfect here on earth before, lest at the lifting up thither it be not able there to abide and so be cast down into the deep dungeon of Hell. The Heavenly Artificer useth many and divers manners in shaping or squaring of stones meet for those walls. Peradventure some be hard and them He must entreat [1] hardly.

We shewed before of Achab: now shall ye hear of Manasses, which was a king of Israel, and followed much Achab in his living. This Manasses ordained and set an idol within the holy place of the Temple, he set up altars of Baal, used witches, charms, and divers other divinations, wherewith Almighty God was very much displeased, and gave him warning by His prophets for to amend himself. But he of pride and obstinacy set but little by their threatenings; after the manner of a wicked person when he is overthrown in sin, he despised them. Almighty God seeing Manasses would not be made meet, neither would not be entreated by fair and easy means (as his desire was), used a more sharp way to him. He caused the Babylonians with great power for to make battle and have the victory: that done, they led him fast bound in chains of iron into Babylon; and there he was set in prison, and at last remembered his unkindness done against Almighty God. Wherefore he wept and sorrowed sore, meekly asking forgiveness. Our merciful Lord of His great goodness anon heard graciously his petition. Thus at the last, albeit it was very hard to bring him to pass, he was made a meet lively stone unto the Heavenly Building by very contrition. Mary Magdalene was much more easily brought to frame than he; which by no threatenings or sharp punishments but only for very love of our Saviour Christ was drawn unto contrition. Thus, as we have rehearsed, Almighty God the high Artificer useth many divers means to shape and square His stones here in the earth, in His Church Militant. He of His goodness would every man and woman should be quick stones made ready for that heavenly building; His will is every creature to be saved, as St. Paul saith. There-

[1] treat.

fore our prophet David,which was so abundantly hot with
the fire of charity, (for fire is needful to sacrifice) desired
not only this acceptable sacrifice of a contrite soul for
himself, but also for the health of all other. He sought
not only his own profit, but also the profit of his neighbour
and the honour of God. Wherefore he said *Benigne fac,
Domine, in bona voluntate tua Sion, ut ædificentur muri
Jerusalem*.

Hitherto whatsoever the prophet hath done was for
one of these causes: either it belonged to his own soul's
health, to the profit of his neighbour, or to the laud of
God. First for his neighbour in his prayer he desired
spiritum rectum, for himself *spiritum sanctum*, and for
the honour of God *spiritum principalem*. Also his desire was to be endued with the Holy Ghost because he
might teach other that err, the right way to Heaven;
which concerneth his neighbour. For himself he asked
to be clean delivered from the corrupt bloods of sin. And
lastly for Almighty God his petition was ever to laud
and praise Him. Furthermore he studied busily to give
unto Almighty God the sacrifice of a sorrowful spirit and
contrite heart for himself. He desired the same to be
performed in other for to finish the walls of Heavenly
Jerusalem, that is for his neighbour. And now lastly he
sheweth all that to be done in the laud and praise of
Almighty God, speaking unto Him thus: *Tunc acceptabis
sacrificium justitiæ, oblationes et holocausta: tunc imponent super altare tuum vitulos:* like as he might say,
" when that Heavenly City of the Church Triumphant is
built and perfectly finished, then, Blessed Lord, shall be
all-whole laud and praise to Thee of all Thy citizens."
Whatsoever sacrifice was done in the Old Law signified
the manner of sacrifice in the New Law of grace. The
sacrifice done in this New Law betokened the very truth
in the Eternal Law of very joy and glory. Among the
Jews in the Old Law were certain oblations and sacrifices
which be now utterly fordone: they be no more pleasing
to Almighty God. There be also in this New Law certain sacrifices and oblations, as we have shewed, but they
shall not ever endure. For in Heaven may be no soul

troubled, neither contrition of heart: as St. John saith
in the Apocalypse. Also we cannot be so clean and pure
in this life to make oblation as we should be. All our
life here we be sprinkled with the dust of sin. For all
be sinners: if we say contrary, no truth is in us. But at
our coming and translation into Heavenly Jerusalem we
shall be made so constant and steadfast by grace that
never after we shall sin deadly or venially. Therefore
our prophet saith *Tunc acceptabis sacrificium justitiæ,
oblationes et holocausta; tunc imponent super altare tuum
vitulos:* " Blessed Lord, then Thou shalt accept our sacrifice of rightwiseness, at that time our oblations and sacrifices shall be pleasant unto Thee." For why? They
shall be clean and pure without spot of sin. Then shall
all Thy well beloved people make acceptable sacrifice
not of fleshly or golden calves, as was in the Old Law,
but of everlasting praisings and lauds, as the prophet
Osee remembereth. We shall without end give thankings
immortal unto Thee in eternal glory: whereunto Thou
bring us by the merits of Thy Son Jesus Christ, that
suffered Passion for all sinners upon a Cross. Amen.

Printed in the USA
CPSIA information can be obtained
at www.ICGtesting.com
LVHW052228140224
771908LV00029B/1273

9 781461 174219